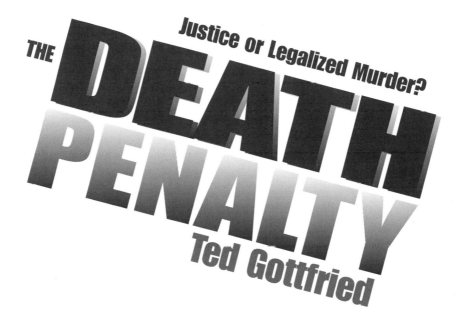

Justice or Legalized Murder?

THE **DEATH PENALTY**

Ted Gottfried

Twenty-First Century Books
Brookfield, Connecticut

Published by Twenty-First Century Books
A Division of The Millbrook Press, Inc.
2 Old New Milford Road
Brookfield, Connecticut 06804
www.millbrookpress.com

Library of Congress Cataloging-in-Publication Data
Gottfried, Ted.
The death penalty : justice or legalized murder? / Ted Gottfried.
p. cm.
Includes bibliographical references and index.
ISBN 0-7613-2155-1 (lib. bdg.)
1. Capital punishment—United States—Juvenile literature. [1.
Capital punishment.] I. Title.
KF9227.C2 G683 2002   364.66'2973—dc21
2001027536

Photographs courtesy of Corbis/Sygma: pp. 17 (© Andrew
Lichtenstein), 20 (© Ron Kuntz), 87 (left © Bishop's Photography;
right © Rodney Freeman/Jonesboro Sun); AP/Wide World Photos:
pp. 27, 43, 60, 69, 73, 105; Photofest: p. 29; © Bettmann/Corbis: pp. 30,
103; MVFR: p. 49; Liaison Agency: pp. 75 (© Phillippe Diederich), 94
(© Lisa Terry); Corbis: p. 106 (© Mark Jenkinson)

Acknowledgments

My gratitude to the personnel of the New York Central Research Library, the Mid-Manhattan Library, the Epiphany Branch Library, and the central branch of the Queensboro Public Library for their aid in researching material. Thanks also to those at Amnesty International, Murder Victims Families for Reconciliation, and Justice For All for their cooperation in providing material for this book. Gratitude is also due my friend and fellow writer Kathryn Paulsen for her support.

Their help was invaluable, but any shortcomings in the work are mine alone.

—Ted Gottfried

For Harriet—
who taught me to love libraries,
and one very special librarian in particular.

Contents

One
The Gathering Storm   11

Two
Public Opinion and the Law   24

Three
An Eye for an Eye   36

Four
Vengeance Is Not Justice   46

Five
Are Innocent People Executed?   56

Six
The Justice System   66

Seven
Too Young to Die?   82

Eight
Is Capital Punishment Biased?   92

Nine
Carrying Out the Sentence   101

Afterword   113
Chronology   117
Chapter Notes   121
Glossary   135
For Further Information   139
Index   141

One
THE GATHERING STORM

My object all sublime
I shall achieve in time—
To let the punishment fit the crime.
The punishment fit the crime . . .[1]
—Song of the Lord High Executioner
from *The Mikado*
by William Schwenck Gilbert

John Michael Lamb was executed by lethal injection in the state prison at Huntsville, Texas, at 6:13 P.M. on November 17, 1999. He said he was sorry for the murder he had committed. He said that he wished he could bring the victim back, but "I can't." He said, "Good-bye. Do it." Those were his last words.[2]

Confession of a Murderer

A week before his sentence was carried out, John Lamb was interviewed by public-radio producers David Isay and Stacy Abramson. He told them he'd had an unhappy life. He said his stepfather beat him. He mentioned that he had attempted suicide when he was nine years old. Then he described his crime.

He told how he had just gotten out of jail in Arkansas where he had served one hundred days for receiving stolen property. He said that the authorities transported him to the state line and warned him not to come back to Arkansas. In Texas, he told the interviewers, he stumbled upon a shed off Interstate 30. There were firearms stored in the shed and he helped himself to two handguns. Subsequently, he was offered a lift from a man who said he had to move some belongings from his room first and asked Lamb to help him. Lamb claimed that when they went to the room, the man made a pass at him. According to Lamb, when he rejected the man's pass, the man got angry and told Lamb to leave. That's when Lamb shot him with one of the two handguns.

"I don't remember pulling the gun out of my pocket," Lamb told the interviewers, "but I know I did—there's no doubt about that. I remember he was trying to hand me his wallet. I knocked the wallet out of his hand and said, 'I don't want that.' And I started shooting. There wasn't no blood, but he lay down and he died. Shot punctured his lung and he drowned in his blood. I don't know why I shot the guy. . . . It was almost as if I was shooting my bad luck or something."[3]

Public Opinion

Do most Americans favor the death penalty for killers like John Michael Lamb? Polls taken in 1999 consistently showed support of about three to one for the death penalty in capital cases. (A capital case is one in which the crime involved is premeditated, and there are no extenuating circumstances. It is punishable by death.) More recently, a June 2000 poll by *Newsweek* magazine found that 73 percent of 750 people polled nationally were in favor of executing murderers.[4] Nevertheless, death penalty opponents believe that public opinion may be changing.

They believe that Americans' answers to polls on capital punishment depend on how the question is asked. Another poll taken in 2000 by the Gallup Organization asked if the penalty for first-degree murder—a capital crime—should be death, or "life imprisonment with absolutely no possibility of parole." Only 56 percent of those responding were for death, while 38 percent favored life sentences without parole. When a Public Policy Institute of California poll of 2,007 Californians put the question the same way, the responses were equally divided between death sentences and sentences of life without parole.[5]

If there is a shift away from approval of capital punishment, it may be because of doubts recently cast on the guilt of some of those who have been put to death. The *Newsweek* poll found that 82 percent of those who responded believed that "at least a few innocent people have been executed since the '70s."[6] The concern is that more innocent people may be among the 3,652 who were awaiting execution on death rows in U.S. prisons as of January 1, 2000.[7]

Until recently, Ronald Williamson was one of those death-row inmates. He had been convicted of "raping, strangling, and mutilating a 21-year-old waitress, Debra Sue Carter, in Oklahoma in 1982." The conviction was based on testimony by Glenn Gore and on strands of hair found at the crime scene. Appeals on Mr. Williamson's behalf delayed his execution. Then, in 1997, DNA sampling determined that the hair came from Glenn Gore, the witness who had testified against

Williamson. This proved Williamson was innocent. Ronald Williamson was released in 1999 after spending eleven years on death row. He was one of the nation's eighty-two death-row inmates whose convictions were reversed—who were found not guilty and released from prison—between 1976 and August 1999. During that time, a total of 566 others were executed. How many of them, capital punishment opponents ask, may have been innocent?[8]

Two Governors Disagree

That question is what lies behind the work of David Protess, a Northwestern University journalism professor, and sixteen of his students. These undergraduates do the legwork for the Center for Wrongful Convictions and the Death Penalty, which is headed by Protess and Professor Lawrence Marshall. Investigations by those connected with the center were responsible for proving the innocence of seven inmates on death row in Illinois and for their release.

Six other convictions of prisoners awaiting execution on Illinois's death row have also been overturned since the state reintroduced capital punishment in 1976, making a total of thirteen. Thirty-three other inmates sentenced to die in Illinois were found to have been represented by lawyers who have been disbarred or suspended according to an investigation by the *Chicago Tribune*. In January 2000, Illinois Governor George H. Ryan, a Republican who supports capital punishment, announced that he was putting a stop to all executions in the state because the system was "fraught with errors."[9] He added that "until I can be sure that everyone sentenced to death in Illinois is truly guilty, until I can be sure with moral certainty that no innocent man or woman is facing a lethal injection, no one will meet the fate."[10]

The moratorium by Governor Ryan focused attention on sentences of death in other states. At the beginning of 2000, thirty-eight states had capital punishment laws. The District of Columbia and twelve states— Alaska, Hawaii, Iowa, Maine, Massachusetts, Michigan, Minnesota, North Dakota, Rhode Island, Vermont, West Virginia, and Wisconsin—did not.[11] Following the Illinois moratorium, the legislatures and/or governors of nine other states—Indiana, Kentucky, Maryland, New Jersey, Oklahoma, Oregon, Pennsylvania, Washington, and New Hampshire—were considering similar measures.

In New Hampshire the state senate passed a bill on May 18, 2000, ending capital punishment. Stronger than a moratorium, which calls only for a halt in executions while capital punishment is studied, the New Hampshire ban would have been the first such action taken by any state since the United States Supreme Court declared capital punishment legal in 1976. However, New Hampshire Governor Jeanne Shaheen, a Democrat, disagreed with the senate, saying "there are some murders so heinous that the death penalty is an appropriate punishment and, accordingly, I will veto this legislation."[12] There was not enough of a majority in the senate to overturn her veto. Twenty-five other governors of death penalty states agreed with Governor Shaheen, "vowing to stamp out any new abolition movements in their states."[13]

The Columbia Study

The capital punishment debate heated up when a Columbia University Law School study was released in June 2000. *The New York Times* described it as "the most far-reaching study of the death penalty in the United States." Written by a team headed by Professor James Liebman and entitled "A Broken System: Error Rates in Capital Cases," the report found that death sentences had been set aside on appeal in 68 percent of convictions between 1973 and 1995. It added that there was "grave doubt whether we do catch" all of the errors.[14]

Champions of the death penalty thought the implication that "we might well be killing many innocent people" was unfair. James Q. Wilson, author of *Moral Judgment* and of *The Moral Sense*, pointed out that the report offered no evidence "that any innocent person has been put to death." He criticized the report for only following up on 301 of the cases that were sent back to the courts to be retried. He pointed out that in these retrials only 22 found the defendant not guilty, while 54 again imposed the death sentence and 247 resulted in lesser prison sentences. His point is that the overwhelming majority were once again found guilty of murder even if most of their sentences were reduced.[15]

A point previously made by David Botkins of the Virginia attorney general's office popped up again in the wake of the Columbia study. Botkins's view is that "the inmates who have been granted clemency and had their death sentences commuted show the system works."[16] How well it works is a question that would be faced by the nation's leading politicians as the 2000 election races gathered momentum.

A Political Issue Emerges

At the beginning of the year all four of the leading presidential candidates—Democrats Vice President Al Gore and former New Jersey Senator Bill Bradley, and

Capital punishment became a hot topic during the 2000 presidential campaign. Some of the attention was focused on Republican candidate George W. Bush. During his time as governor of Texas, Bush had presided over more executions than any other governor in the United States since the Supreme Court reinstated the death penalty in 1976. Death penalty opponents demonstrated outside the Republican National Convention in Philadelphia on July 31, 2000.

Republicans Governor George W. Bush of Texas and Arizona Senator John McCain—favored the death penalty. President Bill Clinton not only favored it, but interrupted his campaign for his party's presidential nomination in 1992 to return to Arkansas where, as governor of the state, he signed papers allowing the execution of a brain-damaged murderer to be carried out. Hillary Clinton, campaigning to represent New York State in the Senate, also favored capital punishment, as did her opponent, Republican congressman Rick Lazio.

After nailing down their parties' nominations, presidential hopefuls Bush and Gore found their positions on the issue being scrutinized. The Illinois moratorium and the release of the Columbia study were followed by a request from Democratic Senator Russ Feingold of Wisconsin to President Clinton that there be a moratorium on federal executions. The request resulted in wide newspaper coverage of the bill introduced by Feingold in the Senate in November 1999, which was designed to abolish the federal death penalty and calling on all states to stop executions. In the wake of this and other protests against capital punishment by organizations and individuals, including the American Bar Association, Pat Robertson, founder of the Christian Broadcasting Network, numerous members of the clergy, and others, the death penalty was pushed to the forefront as a political issue in an election year.

Despite mounting pressure, Gore stuck to his pro-death penalty position, insisting in July 2000 that "I have not yet seen evidence that to me would justify a nation-wide moratorium."[17] In August, *The New York Times/CBS News* polls of Democratic convention delegates and registered Democratic voters found a gap between Gore's position and theirs. Only 20 percent of the delegates and 46 percent of the voters favored the death penalty over life imprisonment. For Republicans the results were 55 percent of the voters and 60 percent of the delegates preferring capital punishment.[18]

While Bush's death penalty views were closer to those of his fellow Republicans than Gore's were to his fellow Democrats, the issue had become more of a problem for Bush than for Gore. By mid-June 2000, as governor of Texas he had presided over 134 executions, more than any other governor in any other state since the Supreme Court restored the death penalty in 1976. "I'm confident that every person that has been put to death in Texas, under my watch, has been guilty of the crime charged," Bush told the NBC news program *Meet the Press*.[19] Nevertheless, his record made him a prime target for death penalty opponents. The magazine *The Nation* labeled him "the Lone Star State's serial-killer governor."[20]

Woman on Death Row

The case of Karla Faye Tucker, who confessed to two killings, had focused the nation's attention on Governor Bush and the death penalty as early as 1998. After a death-row conversion to Christianity, Ms. Tucker had married the prison chaplain and become a model inmate. Evangelical Christians regarded her reform as "proof of the transforming power of God." She appeared on the Larry King TV show and asked Governor Bush to spare her life. There were pleas from the United Nations, the European Parliament, Amnesty International, *Dead Man Walking* author Sister Helen Prejean, Bianca Jagger, and the pope, as well as other religious leaders of many faiths asking that her execution be halted. Nevertheless, Governor Bush allowed the execution to proceed. He later wrote in his autobiography that he had felt "like a huge piece of concrete was crushing

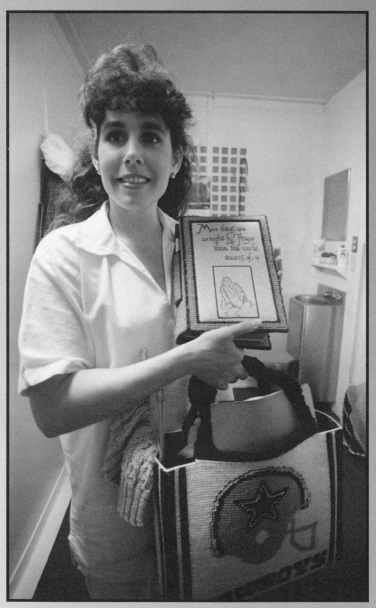

Karla Faye Tucker two months before her execution in February 1998

me" as he waited for the sentence to be carried out. He described it as "the longest twenty minutes of my tenure as governor."[21]

Many who favor the death penalty felt that Bush was unfairly portrayed by the media as callous because the person executed was a woman. They pointed out that if women are to have equal rights with men, then they must bear equal responsibility for their crimes. It was their belief that gender should not be a consideration in carrying through death penalty verdicts.

Opponents of capital punishment do not, however, rest their case on gender. They believe that no person should be executed, male or female. They later rallied around Gary Graham, the Texas death-row prisoner who became as much—possibly more—of a thorn in the side of presidential candidate Bush than Karla Faye Tucker had been.

The Gary Graham Case

Gary Graham was convicted of slaying Bobby Lambert in a parking lot outside a Safeway supermarket in Houston at about 9:30 on the evening of May 13, 1981. Graham was seventeen years old at the time of the killing. He was convicted on the basis of testimony from one witness, Bernadine Skillern, who said she saw him kill Lambert through her car windshield from a distance of thirty to forty feet. Graham was defended by Ronald Mock who, according to *The New York Times*, "put on virtually no defense." Graham had been carrying a gun, but tests determined that it was not the murder weapon. Two other witnesses who claimed to have seen the killer said that it was not Graham. Defense counsel Mock never called them to testify at Graham's trial.[22]

As a presidential candidate, Governor Bush became the focus of pressure from death penalty opponents to prevent the execution of Gary Graham. This intensified when the U.S. Supreme Court voted 5 to 4 not to intervene in Graham's case.[23] When pleas were made to Bush to grant a thirty-day reprieve to Graham, he refused. He said he couldn't act because his predecessor, Texas Governor Ann Richards, had granted the prisoner a reprieve in 1993. According to Bush, the law forbade a second reprieve. He said only the Texas Board of Pardons and Paroles could grant clemency to Graham. The eighty-member board had been appointed by Bush. A leniency recommendation from Bush could influence its decision. Since the board had granted only one clemency appeal of the sixty-eight filed by death-row inmates since 1995, it seemed unlikely that they would grant Graham's without such a recommendation.[24]

The governor declined to intercede. The board rejected Graham's appeal. Bush stressed his duty as governor "to uphold the laws of the land." He explained his position. "I also keep in mind the victims," he said. "And the reason I support the death penalty is I believe it saves lives."[25]

Politics and Passions

Gary Graham was led out of his death-row cell at 8:20 P.M. on Thursday, June 22, 2000. According to a spokesperson for the Texas Department of Criminal Justice, he struggled and it took five guards to subdue him and strap him to the gurney. His final words were: "They are killing me tonight. They are murdering me."

As Governor Bush pointed out, over a period of nineteen years the Graham death sentence had been reviewed "more than twenty times by state and federal courts."[26] More than thirty-three judges had been involved in these reviews. Six days before the execution, witness Bernadine Skillern repeated her testimony that she had seen "Mr. Graham shoot and kill Mr. Lambert on that parking lot in 1981."[27]

It is difficult, in the opinion of those who favor the death penalty, to make the case that the system failed Graham. Nor is there any evidence that Governor (subsequently President) Bush's rival candidate for the presidency, Democrat Al Gore, would have taken a different position in the case of Gary Graham. Capital punishment may well take center stage as a political issue in the future, but it is an issue that cuts across party lines. It is a gut-level issue, an issue of the heart as well as the mind.

Two
PUBLIC OPINION AND THE LAW

No question is ever settled
Until it is settled right.[1]
    —From a poem by Ella Wheeler Wilcox

The history of capital punishment in the United States demonstrates how public opinion can influence the law in a democracy. It is a seesaw history with American society alternately demanding the death penalty and rejecting it. The courts, particularly the United States Supreme Court, have at different times used the Eighth Amendment to the Constitution, which bans "cruel and unusual punishments," to justify both of these opposing viewpoints.[2]

To Kill or Not to Kill?

Both the death penalty and campaigns against it have been part of our nation's history since its beginnings. Following British law, execution was a punishment approved by most of the leaders of the new nation. It was first denounced during colonial times by Dr. Benjamin Rush, founder of the anti-capital punishment movement in this country. One of the few founding fathers to support Dr. Rush's movement was Benjamin Franklin.

The movement did not gain much support until 1840, when the *New York Tribune* publisher and presidential candidate, Horace Greeley, campaigned against capital punishment. In 1847, Michigan became the first state to abolish the death penalty. Rhode Island and Wisconsin followed. After the Civil War, Maine and Iowa ended the death penalty, and then restored it. Maine did away with it again in 1887.

This frequently shifting policy was followed by many states, and by the federal government as well, over the years which followed. In the 1880s the federal government decreed that only murder, treason, and rape could be punished by death. When Colorado abolished the death penalty, lynchings followed, and it was restored. Between 1907 and 1917, nine states and Puerto Rico did away with capital punishment. By 1921, five of these states had brought it back.

Between 1917 and 1957 none of the states ended capital punishment. In 1947 executions in the United States reached a high for the decade of 152. However, that trend was about to change drastically.

Cell 2455, Death Row

In 1948, twenty-seven-year-old Caryl Chessman confessed to being the Red-Light Bandit. Newspapers had given the culprit this name because he would drive a car flashing a red light resembling that of a police vehicle and approach couples parked in lonely spots. He would rob the driver and then force the woman to drive off with him and perform sexual acts. Chessman later claimed his confession had been obtained through torture by the police.[3]

The jury didn't believe Chessman. They found him guilty. They made no recommendation of mercy. Chessman was sentenced under a California law that provided for the death penalty in cases of kidnapping "with bodily harm." He was condemned to die in the gas chamber on March 28, 1952.[4]

Poring over law books without outside legal aid, Chessman filed an appeal and obtained a stay (temporary delay) of execution. He then wrote a book called *Cell 2455, Death Row.* Published in 1954, it sold half a million copies and was translated into a dozen languages.

Chessman used the proceeds from *Cell 2455, Death Row* to hire lawyers. They filed further appeals on his behalf for the next six years. During that time, according to the *Encyclopedia of Crime*, his case "produced one of the most intense anti-capital punishment campaigns in history. . . . Protests came from all levels of society. Millions of persons in Brazil, 2.5 million in São Paulo alone, and thousands more in Switzerland signed petitions pleading for his life." Many of these people believed the punishment excessive because even if Chessman was guilty, he had not murdered anyone. Among those who pleaded for him were the queen of Belgium, Eleanor Roosevelt, evangelist Billy Graham, author Norman Mailer, actor Marlon Brando, and poet Robert Frost. Their pleas were in vain. The Democratic governor of California, Edmund G. Brown, although claiming to be opposed to the death penalty, either would not or could not save Chessman. Chessman was executed in the San Quentin gas chamber on May 2, 1960.[5]

Caryl Chessman, two days before his execution, holds another book he wrote during his twelve years on death row, The Kid Was a Killer.

I Want to Live

Following Chessman's death, public distaste for capital punishment grew. It was fueled by the 1958 movie, *I Want to Live*. The film was described by movie historian Leslie Halliwell as a "sober, harrowing treatment of the Barbara Graham case." It was viewed by Halliwell as part of "the tirade against capital punishment" being heard at that time.[6]

Actress Susan Hayward played Barbara Graham in a performance that earned her an Academy Award. The film focused on Graham's time on death row, during which she was on the brink of execution time after time only to be saved by court orders. In the end, in the film, like Chessman, Hayward as Graham is executed in the San Quentin gas chamber.

The film did not exactly say Barbara Graham was innocent, but it was designed to create maximum sympathy for her. Her unsavory past was hinted at, but the movie didn't go into its details. Her actual crime was glossed over.

In fact, Barbara Graham was a sometime prostitute who, in March 1953, together with a gang of four men, set out to rob a sixty-two-year-old crippled Burbank, California, widow. Graham rang the widow's doorbell and asked to use the telephone. When the woman opened the door, Graham's four accomplices crowded into the living room behind her. Graham then struck the widow, grabbed her by the hair, and beat her over the head with the butt of a gun. She cracked the skull of the old woman, killing her. Graham was convicted of the crime and her real-life execution took place in June 1955.[7]

The brutality of Graham's crime was never made clear in the film. Rather, it was Hayward's death-row

Susan Hayward as Barbara Graham
in the 1958 film I Want to Live

Barbara Graham arrives at San Quentin prison in California the day before her execution.

performance that swayed public attitudes against capital punishment. Following the nationwide release of *I Want to Live,* there was a notable decrease in executions in the United States. Alaska, Hawaii, and Delaware abolished the death penalty. Although Delaware restored it three years later, the trend toward ending capital punishment continued through the late 1950s into the 1960s.

Abolishing the Death Penalty

There were only 7 executions in the United States in 1965, as compared with the 152 that had been carried out in 1947. By 1967 there were just 2. The states' reluctance to execute death-row prisoners reflected studies showing that "in 1967 public opinion was overwhelmingly opposed to the death penalty."[8] The following year saw a nationwide suspension of capital punishment, which lasted nine years.

One of the main reasons for the suspension was that the United States Supreme Court had been influenced by society's attitudes. A series of anti-capital punishment lawsuits brought in the late 1960s resulted in a succession of vaguely worded Supreme Court decisions, which effectively prevented states from carrying through death sentences even if they wanted to do so. Then, in 1972, the Supreme Court ruled that "capital punishment laws, as enforced, were unconstitutional."[9] In the Court's judgment, they involved the very "cruel and unusual punishments" that were banned by the Eighth Amendment to the Constitution.[10] Justice William J. Brennan, voting with the majority, found that the death penalty's "rejection by contemporary society is virtually total."[11]

Restoring Capital Punishment

One of those voting against abolishing the death penalty in 1972 was Justice Lewis Powell. A year earlier Justice Powell had been named to the court by President Richard Nixon. During his time on the court he always supported capital punishment.

This was true in 1976 when the Supreme Court restored the death penalty after nine years of disuse. During the four years between the two Supreme Court capital punishment decisions, the traffic in illegal drugs had caused an alarming rise in crimes of violence. Murder rates were high and mounting. Poll after poll revealed that public opinion had shifted dramatically to favor the death penalty.

Justice Powell voted with the majority in 1976 in the case of *Gregg* v. *Georgia* and two other cases. A 7 to 2 decision upheld death sentences and found that "the infliction of death as a punishment for murder is not without justification and thus is not unconstitutionally severe."[12] In effect the Court had decided that death did not fit the definition of "cruel and unusual punishments" forbidden by the Eighth Amendment to the Constitution.[13]

"Let's Do It!"

In 1977 the first man to be executed in ten years was thirty-six-year-old Gary Gilmore. He was a self-hating career criminal who had been convicted in Utah of murdering a gas-station attendant and a motel clerk. When attempts were made to block his execution, Gilmore "disparaged groups and individuals opposed to capital punishment." He was killed by a five-man firing squad on January 17, 1977, in the Utah State Prison. His last words were: "Let's do it!"[14]

In a strange way Gilmore was reflecting the public attitude, which had shifted heavily in favor of capital punishment. Norman Mailer's book about Gilmore, *Executioner's Song*, was not designed to raise sympathy for him, nor to affect attitudes toward the death penalty one way or the other. Public attitudes were, however, increasingly influenced in favor of capital punishment by the escalating violence throughout the country.

Throughout the 1980s, as concern for public safety grew, so too did support of the sternest measures to punish brutal crimes. During the 1990s, acts of terrorism like the Oklahoma City Federal Building bombing, the bombing of the World Trade Center in New York City, and the bombings of abortion clinics across the country solidified this support. The public came to believe that executing murderers was the most effective way to protect their own lives. The reality of increasing and often fatal violence created a very real and personal fear for one's own safety and the safety of one's family and friends. Approval of capital punishment became firmly grounded in that fear.

Justice Powell's About-Face

In 1987 the Supreme Court had heard the case of *McCleskey* v. *Kemp*. Warren McCleskey, a black man, had been convicted of two counts of armed robbery and one count of murder. His victim had been a white police officer. A Georgia court sentenced McCleskey to death. The Georgia Supreme Court affirmed the convictions and the death sentence.[15]

McCleskey's appeal to the United States Supreme Court was based on a survey, which showed that "defendants charged with killing white victims in Georgia are 4.3 times as likely to be sentenced to death as defendants charged with killing blacks."[16] The Court rejected this argument by a vote of 5 to 4 and denied McCleskey's appeal. Justice Lewis Powell wrote the opinion for the majority. In it he observed that "apparent disparities in sentencing are an inevitable part of our criminal justice system."[17] McCleskey was subsequently executed.

Later that year Justice Powell retired from the Supreme Court. A few years after his retirement, he was asked if there was any case he had second thoughts about. His answer was *"McCleskey* v. *Kemp."* Then, considering his record on the court, former Justice Lewis Powell made a remarkable statement. "I have come to think that capital punishment should be abolished," he said.[18]

Justice Powell's about-face, however, was out of step with the majority of Americans. Lawmakers, in part responding to polls confirming that the public's pro-capital punishment attitudes were hardening, acted accordingly. Following a 1989 Supreme Court decision in *Murray* v. *Giarratano* that "there is no constitutional right to counsel in state post-conviction proceedings," Congress cut off funding for twenty Death Penalty Resource Centers. The centers had handled appeals for death-row prisoners who could not afford to hire lawyers. Over the next few years, some states also cut support for such appeals.[19]

In 1994 the Federal Death Penalty Act authorized capital punishment for more than sixty federal offenses, "including some crimes that do not involve murder."[20] The Anti-terrorism and Effective Death Penalty Act, signed into law by President Clinton in 1996, severely limited the number of appeals allowed by law in death penalty cases and placed a time limit of one year on the filing of such appeals.[21] It would be the dawning of the twenty-first century, more than twenty years after the Gilmore execution, before there would be signs that the pendulum might be swinging back again.

Three
AN EYE FOR AN EYE

*He that smiteth a man, so that he die,
shall be surely put to death.*[1]
                    —Chapter 21, Verse 12,
                    Exodus, *Holy Bible*

Sixteen-year-old Shari Ann Merton was murdered in 1983 and her killer, Corey R. Barton, accepted a plea bargain, which resulted in his serving just nine years and eight months in prison. In November 1998, Barton was charged with a second murder, that of twenty-seven-year-old Sally Harris. He was one of many killers, say proponents of capital punishment, who go free and kill again. They add that when the death penalty is enforced, that doesn't happen. "By executing murderers," they point out, " you prevent them from murdering again and . . . save innocent life."[2]

Those who favor capital punishment point out that killers have proven by their acts that they are violent people. Situations which most people would respond to with anger are responded to by killers with rage.

Sometimes the rage is uncontrollable. Sometimes that rage is an emotion they carry around with them all their lives; it is a volcanic emotion waiting for an opportunity to erupt.

The Killer Writer

The most famous case that cast the gravest doubts on whether it was possible to rehabilitate violent killers was that of thirty-seven-year-old Jack Henry Abbott. Behind bars on and off since the age of twelve, Abbott was serving a sentence for passing bad checks when he murdered a fellow inmate. Described by prison psychiatrists as "a potentially dangerous man with a hair-trigger temper," Abbott had spent years in solitary confinement because of his violent nature.[3]

When Abbott read that Norman Mailer was writing a book about convicted murderer Gary Gilmore and his upcoming execution, he contacted the renowned author and offered to give him a crash course in the realities of prison life. Impressed with Abbott's raw talent as a writer, Mailer took him up on the offer. Their correspondence led Mailer to enlist writers, editors, and publishers of the New York literary establishment to join him in petitioning the Utah parole board to grant Abbott early release. When Random House gave Abbott a book contract with a $12,500 advance, he was let out of prison and assigned to a halfway house in New York.

There was no doubt that he possessed an impressive talent. His book *In the Belly of the Beast* received mostly rave reviews. Abbott was a gifted writer. Nevertheless, he was still a killer.

In a New York City bar called the Binibon, Abbott got into an argument with a waiter over using the men's room. The part-time waiter, a recently married twenty-

"Awesome, brilliant...the most intense, the most fiercely visionary book of its kind in the American repertoire of prison literature." —*The New York Times Book Review*

LETTERS FROM PRISON

IN THE BELLY OF THE BEAST

JACK HENRY ABBOTT

WITH AN INTRODUCTION BY NORMAN MAILER

Jack Henry Abbott's book

two-year-old aspiring actor and playwright named Richard Adan tried to explain to Abbott that the policy of the Binibon was to limit use of the men's room to customers only. Abbott wasn't a customer, and when he began causing a scene, Adan went outside with him to try to calm him down. In the alley Abbott pulled a knife and stabbed Adan, killing him.[4]

"Lifers" Who Murder

Jack Henry Abbott is not unique, say proponents of the death penalty. Life imprisonment too often does not remove the danger of murderers killing again. Even if he never goes free, the violent murderer is a threat to his fellow prisoners and to those who guard him. A perceived insult, lack of respect, or unfairness may trigger his or her violence. It is a part of the murderer's character, buried deep inside, a time bomb waiting to go off.

Bennie Demps, they say, was just such a time bomb. In May 2000, Demps lost an appeal before the Florida Supreme Court and was scheduled to be executed the following week. Demps had originally been sentenced to death for two murders committed in 1971. He had stolen a safe and was hiding out in a citrus grove when Nicholas and Celia Puhlick and R. N. Brinkworth stumbled on him. Demps fatally shot Celia Puhlik and Brinksworth and wounded Nicholas Puhlik. Demps was saved from execution in 1972 when the United States Supreme Court found capital punishment to be unconstitutional. Demps was removed from death row and held with the general prison population. In September 1976, two months after the Court reversed itself and upheld Florida's new capital punishment law, Demps took part in the fatal stabbing of another inmate. The inmate named him before he died. In 1978 Demps was sentenced to death for this murder. Appeals delayed carrying out the sentence for twenty-two more years.[5]

More than the threat to fellow prisoners, however, capital punishment proponents are concerned about the danger murderers pose to those charged with enforcing the discipline that inmates must live by. They point to the March 2000 indictment for murder of twenty-year-old Robert Lynn Pruett as evidence of how prison personnel are at risk from convicted killers. Pruett was serving a life term at the Texas Department of Criminal Justice McConnell unit for a murder he committed when he was fifteen years old. It is alleged that he held down prison guard Daniel Nagle while another prisoner fatally stabbed Nagle with a sharpened steel rod. If convicted, this time Pruett faces the death chamber. Were that not so, death penalty advocates point out, "lifers" like Pruett already would be serving the ultimate sentence and there would be no deterrence to their killing again.

Death Sentences Are a Deterrent

Republican Senator Arlen Specter of Pennsylvania became convinced that "the death penalty is a deterrent to crime" during his twelve years of service with the Philadelphia District Attorney's Office. He writes of many cases "where robbers and burglars avoid carrying weapons for fear a gun or knife will be used in a murder, subjecting them to the death penalty."[6] Writing in *Forbes* magazine, Steven E. Landsburg points out that "for thirty years the economics journals have been publishing evidence for large deterrent effects when death penalties are enforced."[7] A study by University of Chicago Professor Isaac Ehrlich indicated that "eight murders were deterred by every execution."[8]

The belief that the death penalty will deter people from committing murder rests on the simple psychological truth that most people would rather live than die. Retired Professor Ernest van den Haag, formerly of Fordham University Law School and New York University, points out that "most people fear death a great deal" and therefore "most people would choose almost any type of life, including life in prison, over death."[9] Advocates of capital punishment insist that the prospect of being executed will make criminals think twice before adding murder to their other crimes.

Those who support the death penalty add that the fact that "99.9 percent of all convicted capital murderers and their attorneys argue for life, not death, in the punishment phase of their trial" (the hearing that takes place after conviction to decide on what their sentence should be) proves that the prospect of capital punishment fills them with fear. They claim that if executions were carried out more swiftly, "the effect of deterrence will rise." Prisoners themselves, they say, "rate the death penalty as the most feared punishment, much more so than life without parole."[10]

The Case for Vengeance

Some advocates of capital punishment justify it more harshly. Professor van den Haag, long a leader of the pro-death penalty movement, reminds us that "Nature has sentenced us all to death. Execution hastens, but does not create the unavoidable end of human life. What makes execution different is that it brands the executed as morally unworthy to belong to human society." He adds that "the paramount moral purpose of punishment is retributive justice."[11]

While "retributive justice" has been understood as code words for vengeance, some offenses are viewed as so horrible that many death penalty advocates do not shy away from the notion. They point to crimes like that of Allen Lee Davis who was put to death in Florida's electric chair in July 1999. Davis had broken into the home of the Weiler family in Jacksonville, Florida, while Mr. Weiler was away on a business trip. He attacked thirty-seven-year-old Nancy Weiler. She was three-months pregnant when he bludgeoned her to death with a gun. He hit her so hard that he broke the metal frame of the gun. Then Davis tied up ten-year-old Kristy Weiler and shot her in the face, killing her. When five-year-old Kathy Weiler tried to run away, Davis first shot her and then crushed her skull.[12]

Many of those who believe in the death penalty are outraged that Davis was on death row for sixteen years before he was executed. They are appalled that because blood appeared on his shirt at the time of the execution, anti-capital punishment crusaders use his execution as proof that the death penalty is inhumane. Look at the crime, they say, not the punishment. If ever vengeance was justified, they say, it was justified in the case of Allen Lee Davis.

A murder committed by Richard Allen Davis (no relation to Allen Lee Davis) left the victim's father endorsing vengeance via the death penalty. Before Davis kidnapped twelve-year-old Polly Klaas from a slumber party on October 1, 1993, and killed her, Polly's father, Marc Klaas, had believed the death penalty "was cruel and unusual punishment." Now he says he knows "you don't rehabilitate psychopaths." Klaas wants to witness

Polly Klaas

the execution of Davis. "I'd like my eyes to be the last thing he sees," says Klaas, "just as his eyes were the last thing my child saw."[13]

The Need for Closure

Not all survivors of murder victims who are for the death penalty view the issue in terms of retributive justice, or vengeance. They feel that the more pressing justification is closure. They may mean different things by the word, but the one meaning among others that they hold in common is putting an end to the nightmare of the crime responsible for their loss.

"I am relieved. You just can't understand what enormous relief it is that all this is finally over and done with," said Traci Freeman when the murderer of her younger sibling was executed. Betti Shupe, the daughter of a homicide victim, said she was "relieved" by the execution of the murderer because "there's no more worry that he's going to get out."[14] When Wilford Berry was put to death for the slaying of Charles J. Mitroff Jr., the victim's brother-in-law, Richard Bowler, reflected on "a brutal, senseless act committed nine years ago against a good, decent person," and concluded that "at last we have closure."[15]

An anonymous pro-death penalty champion on the Internet regards closure in other terms. "If you had a loved one killed," the writer asks, "and you knew that your tax dollars were being used to keep your child's killer alive, would you not be angry with every dollar you pay for taxes? At least with capital punishment, you know that your tax dollars were used to keep a killer from reentering society, and not to keep a killer alive."[16]

Executing Killers Is Cost Effective

The above is part of the argument in favor of capital punishment, which stands back from considerations of deterrence, repeat offenses, vengeance, and closure to take a more dollars-and-cents approach. It points out that life sentences, the frequently advocated alternative to the death penalty, impose an unreasonable burden on society to feed, house, clothe, and care for murderers. Life without parole for fifty years (based on the average age of convicted killers and their average life expectancy) calculated at present costs of $34,200 per year plus a 2 percent annual cost increase comes to $3.01 million per inmate.[17]

The new laws, which shortened the appeals process in death penalty cases, project an average stay on death row of six years. At $60,000 per year plus a 2 percent annual cost increase, that comes to $1.88 million. Carrying out the death penalty would save society $1.13 million dollars per execution, according to capital punishment proponents.[18]

This money, they point out, might better be spent on schools, health care, and improving the environment. It might provide some genuine benefits to society. It might be used for crime prevention, rather than for prolonging the life of a murderer who, given the opportunity, might well kill again.

Four

VENGEANCE IS NOT JUSTICE

I stand firmly and unequivocally opposed to the death penalty for those convicted of capital offenses. An evil deed is not redeemed by an evil deed of retaliation. Justice is never advanced in the taking of a human life. Morality is never upheld by a legalized murder.[1]
—Coretta Scott King, whose mother-in-law, and whose husband, Reverend Dr. Martin Luther King Jr., were both murder victims

The basic case against capital punishment is summed up by death penalty opponents in four words: "Thou shalt not kill."[2] For some this is a religious conviction. For others it is a moral principle. Either way, it is not concerned with the guilt or innocence of the person being executed. Carrying out the death sentence is wrong because killing is wrong. It is as wrong when the state does it as punishment as when a killer murders a victim.

This is the belief that underlies the arguments used to answer the case made by those who advocate capital punishment. Those who would extend mercy to killers approach almost all discussions of the death penalty differently than those who approve of it. It follows that the view that closure for family members of victims justifies executing their killers is disputed by survivors like Coretta Scott King and others.

Honor the Memory

Since 1976 some of these survivors have belonged to Murder Victims Families for Reconciliation (MVFR), which opposes the death penalty. MVFR was founded by Marie Deans of Richmond, Virginia, following the murder of her mother-in-law. In the early 1990s, Marietta Jaeger, the mother of a slain seven-year-old daughter, was the driving force in turning MVFR into a national organization, which by 2000 would number four thousand members.

Marietta Jaeger's seven-year-old daughter Susie had been kidnapped from a Montana campground on June 25, 1973. The side canvas of the tent in which she had been sleeping with four older siblings had been slashed, and Susie's stuffed animals were strewn on the ground outside. A year after Susie vanished, the kidnapper phoned her mother. Ms. Jaeger tape-recorded the call. "He wanted to taunt me," she remembers. "He said, 'I'm in charge here and you're not.'" He went on to describe his "lonely life"; he "broke down and wept."[3]

Before long, the FBI zeroed in on a suspect in the case. His name was David. (His last name is being withheld out of Marietta Jaeger's concern for his family.) The voice on the phone call tape matched David's. When his home was searched, body parts were discovered in the freezer. They belonged to several women and children who had been missing. Finally David confessed to killing Susie Jaeger. After he cut through the tent, he said, he had choked Susie until she was unconscious. Then he had held the terrified child prisoner for one week before strangling her and dismembering her body.[4]

Marietta Jaeger told Montana state prosecutors that she was opposed to their seeking the death penalty for David. The issue had not been decided when David settled it by hanging himself in his jail cell. The question remained as to why Ms. Jaeger opposed executing her child's murderer. She answered it with these words: "How do we best honor the memory of a loved one? Doesn't she deserve a more beautiful memorial than killing a chained, restrained, defenseless person? How does that provide peace for the victim's family?" Indeed, she adds, "a vindictive mind-set creates bitterness and lets the criminal claim one more victim."[5]

Condemning Innocent Loved Ones

A few of the members of MVFR belong to families of inmates who have been executed. The effect on the relatives of condemned and executed men is considered by death penalty opponents to be punishment of the innocent by an insensitive justice system. "The families of the condemned have to cope with deaths that are both lingering and violent . . . the extent of the damage this inflicts on families, especially upon children, is not yet fully known," according to a Florida study of the relatives of condemned inmates.[6]

MVFR members speak out at a National Coalition to Abolish the Death Penalty conference in Philadelphia in 1999.

Because there is often an extended time lapse between imposing a death sentence and carrying it out, these families "know for years that the state intends to kill their relatives and the method that will be used." This sentences parents, siblings, marriage partners, children, and other relatives to "a prolonged period of anticipatory grieving." They live with the shame that their condemned loved ones "have been formally cast out of society and judged to be unworthy to live."[7]

The sister of a condemned man describes an experience typical of what families of the condemned may encounter. "One day a customer came in who I knew and knew my brother was on death row. Something came on the radio about the death penalty and he said just loud enough so that I could hear, 'All convicts are animals. Do them like you do a dead rabbit.'" The sister excused herself, went in the back of the store, and sobbed out her grief in private.[8]

Executions Brutalize Society

In the eyes of its opponents, the man who made that remark had been brutalized by the death penalty. Capital punishment, they say, has this effect on society as a whole. They say that the message that the state sends when it executes people is that life is cheap. To some unstable people this may mean that it is all right to kill. In this way executions may encourage murder.

Hugo Adam Bedau, former chairman of the board of directors of the National Coalition to Abolish the Death Penalty, and author of many books on the subject, believes that "use of the death penalty in a given state may actually increase the subsequent rate of criminal homicide." He quotes a study in *Criminology* magazine, which found that "the death penalty weakens . . . inhibitions against the use of lethal force to settle disputes."[9] In Bedau's view, the benefits of the death penalty are an illusion while "the bloodshed and the resulting destruction of community decency are real."[10]

It follows that Bedau does not believe that capital punishment is ever a deterrent to murder. He points out that most murders are committed in the heat of the moment, and often by those who are drunk or who have taken drugs. They are in no condition to consider that they may be executed for the act they are about to commit. There is little time between the impulse and the crime to consider the death penalty.

As for slayings committed by terrorists, contract killers, or drug dealers, Bedau and other opponents of the death penalty do not believe such murderers will be deterred by it. "Terrorists," says Bedau, "usually act in the name of an ideology that honors its martyrs." Death means eternal paradise to them. If hit men were afraid of dying, they would not have chosen their life of crime in the first place. Drug dealers are conditioned to risk their lives in competition with other dealers. "It is irrational," writes Bedau, "to think that the death penalty . . . will avert murders committed in drug turf wars or by street-level dealers."[11]

Many law enforcement officials believe that capital punishment is no deterrent to murder. They say that "curbing drug use and putting more officers on the street, longer sentences and gun control" are the methods most effective in reducing violent crime. They find the death penalty "least effective."[12]

Capital Punishment Is Not Consistent

A study of capital punishment by the United Nations agrees. It could not find any evidence that the death

penalty prevented killings.[13] In Europe, eighteen countries have ratified the Sixth Protocol to the European
Convention on Human Rights, which outlaws the death
penalty in peacetime.[14] Today more than half the nations
in the world—106—have either abolished the death
penalty or have not used it in ten years or more.
Included are most of the industrialized nations of the
world. Among the exceptions are China, Egypt, Japan,
South Korea, and the United States.[15] We are the leader
of the free world, say those against capital punishment.
We should be on the side of mercy, not on the side of
death.

They add that the administration of capital punishment is rarely consistent. They point out that when the
states of our nation are compared with each other, their
use of the death penalty varies widely. While the
combined death-row inmate population of California,
Texas, and Florida on January 1, 2001, was 1,426, that of
three states with similar urban crime problems—New
York, Illinois, and Louisiana—totaled only 276. In twelve
other states—among them Massachusetts, Michigan,
and Hawaii—there are no prisoners on death row
because they do not have the death penalty. Capital
punishment, opponents conclude, is more a matter of
where the crime is committed than of justice.[16]

This is borne out by the fact that death penalty
states differ when it comes to carrying out executions.
Between 1977 and September 2000, Texas executed 239
prisoners. Pennsylvania, with 243 prisoners on death
row as of January 1, 2001, had only 3 executions during
that period. The reasons for this, say anti-capital punishment advocates, are the differences in the way the
courts of the two states handle the appeals of death-row
prisoners, as well as the availability of competent attorneys to handle those appeals.[17]

Agony of the Condemned

Death penalty opponents believe that this is a key factor contributing to the risk of executing innocent persons. They often quote Supreme Court Justice William J. Brennan's opinion that "the death penalty is imposed not only in a freakish and discriminatory manner, but also in some cases upon defendants who are actually innocent."[18] According to Amnesty International, the "number of innocent people sentenced to death represents more than one percent of all U.S. death sentences." They claim that "for every six prisoners executed . . . one innocent person was condemned to die and later exonerated."[19]

Guilty or innocent, regardless of the method used, the person who is executed suffers horribly, according to those who oppose the death penalty. In all cases, even those of lethal injection, which is intended to be the most humane means of putting someone to death, there has been witness testimony of unmeasurable agony during the last moments of life. It is a time, advocates say, when physical and mental pain cannot be separated.

The mental pain begins with the sentence of death and may continue for years before the sentence is finally carried out. The death-row experience of hope and disappointment, the end anticipated and then postponed only to be rescheduled, is a mental torture, which ordinary people cannot imagine. If that is not the "cruel and unusual punishment" of the condemned forbidden by the Constitution, ask death penalty opponents, then what is?[20]

Mercy Is Practical

Some of those who are against capital punishment feel that rehabilitation should be considered a possibility for even the most hardened killer. They say that both morality and religion tell us a person may atone, may reform, and even may someday make a contribution to society. They do not advocate that killers be set free, but they do point out that a live criminal may have the potential to change, while a dead one never will.

Such an attitude toward the condemned often leaves opponents of the death penalty open to the charge of being bleeding hearts, impractical souls who lack the toughness needed to fight fire with fire in the real world. They answer this characterization with facts and figures calculated to demonstrate that it is capital punishment which is impractical. They challenge the idea that it is cheaper to execute a condemned person than to sentence one to life without parole.

According to Honolulu prosecuting attorney Peter Carlisle, prosecuting a death penalty case is "extremely expensive."[21] Other opponents of capital punishment claim that "the average cost per execution in the United States (that is, the entire process) ranges about $2 million to $3 million." Death penalty opponents say that the cost of jailing prisoners for life without parole averages only $20,000 per year—roughly a third less than the cost estimated by capital punishment proponents. On that basis, the cost for fifty years is roughly $1 million. They say this makes the death penalty "approximately two to three times more expensive" than life without parole.[22]

The core case against capital punishment is also pragmatic. Advocates cite a combination of government statistics and the results of a September 2000 survey by

The New York Times, which demonstrates that "during the last twenty years, the homicide rate in states with the death penalty has been 48 percent to 101 percent higher than in states without the death penalty."[23] This proves, say opponents, that capital punishment simply doesn't work.

Five

ARE INNOCENT
PEOPLE EXECUTED?

*Since the beginning of the republic we
have accepted the possibility that innocent people will be convicted of capital
crimes and executed. We also accept that
parole and bail will result in additional
crimes, even the murder of innocent
people.*[1]

—February 2, 2000, letter to
The New York Times
from Wade Butler
of San Marcos, Texas

It's safe to say that nobody wants to execute a person
who is innocent. The view of those who favor the death
penalty is that the risk is slight. Those against capital
punishment believe the danger is considerable.

What Price Capital Punishment?

People like Wade Butler and pro-death penalty advocate Professor van den Haag believe that executions of the innocent are few and far between. Professor van den Haag makes this clear even as he insists that "many desirable social practices cannot avoid killing innocents by accident. For instance, ambulances save many lives, but they also run over some pedestrians. We do not abolish ambulances, because they save more innocent people than they kill. So does the death penalty, if it deters some murders, as is likely, and if the miscarriages are few, as is likely too. It seems safer then to rely on executions, which through deterrence may save innocent lives, than it would be not to execute and risk not saving an indefinite number of innocents who could have been saved."[2]

Opponents of capital punishment disagree. They agree with Sir William Blackstone, an eighteenth-century legal scholar who defined the British law upon which United States law is based, that "it is better that ten guilty persons escape than one innocent suffer."[3] They believe that innocent people are too often executed. They believe that the system of justice which condemns human beings to death is so flawed that the execution of the innocent is inevitable. They cite cases to justify this view.

One such case is that of Ellis Wayne Felker, who was executed in Georgia on November 16, 1996, for the 1981 murder of Joy Ludlam. Two months before Felker was put to death, prosecutors admitted they had withheld evidence. Felker, his legs and head already shaved for the electrodes to be used in his electrocution, was granted a stay so that his attorneys could go over the five crates of papers involved in his case, among which the withheld evidence was included. On October 26, 1996, the Georgia Supreme Court refused to consider whether the new evidence might prove his innocence. On November 14, the United States Supreme Court unanimously denied Felker's final appeal. Hours later, Felker died in the electric chair.[4]

Guilty or Not?

How innocent was Ellis Wayne Felker? The body of Joy Ludlam, the victim in the case, was found in a water-filled ditch. The autopsy found she had been dead five days. Felker had been under around-the-clock surveillance by the police in an unrelated matter for the thirteen days prior to the murder—proof, Felker claimed, of his innocence. Despite the autopsy finding, a laboratory technician testified at Felker's trial that the body could have been in the water for fourteen days. However, professional pathologists testified during the appeals process that Joy Ludlam could not have been dead any longer than three days when her body was found.[5]

Michael Bowers, attorney general of Georgia, did not agree with those who believed that the new evidence, which the court refused to review, taken together with the pathologists' reports, proved Felker's innocence. Bowers said that he "talked to the cops who investigated him," and is convinced of Felker's guilt. "There is rarely any doubt about the guilt of these people, virtually none," insisted Bowers. "These guys on death row are the pits," he added.[6]

Those who believe there is reasonable doubt of Ellis Felker's guilt are outraged by what they see as Bowers's insensitivity. They point out that four Georgia death-row prisoners have been found innocent and released since 1976. This is proof, they say, that the system is flawed.[7]

The Ricky McGinn Case

Cases like Ellis Felker's are rare exceptions, say advocates of capital punishment. For one thing, while his guilt may be in doubt, so too is his innocence. The justice system, they insist, is structured to give condemned persons every chance, often over a period of many years, to prove they are innocent. It is only after many appeals have been heard and rejected that the great majority of executions are actually carried out.

They cite the case of Ricky McGinn, who was sentenced to die for the 1993 rape and murder of his twelve-year-old stepdaughter, Stephanie Rae Flanary. McGinn had been found not guilty of a previous murder. He had also previously been accused of rape, but the charges were dropped. His own daughter by a previous marriage said he had molested her, but again he wasn't charged. Finally, McGinn was a suspect in the murders of two women, which had occurred in 1989 and 1992.[8]

The crime for which McGinn was convicted was particularly brutal. The day of the murder, McGinn's wife left her daughter in his care in their home in Brownwood, Texas. McGinn and Stephanie spent the day alone together. She was sexually assaulted and then her head was beaten in with a roofer's hammer. Her body was found three days later in a nearby ditch. Police found a bloody hammer under the seat of McGinn's truck. They also found blood in the trunk of his car. A drop of blood was also found on his shoe and another drop on his shorts. All the blood found matched Stephanie's blood type.[9]

McGinn claimed he was framed. He pointed out "that the bloody hammer wasn't found during repeated searches of his truck by sheriff's deputies, implying that it was planted." He also said that testimony establishing

Ricky McGinn's death sentence was upheld after DNA testing confirmed his guilt seven years after his conviction.

the time of Stephanie's death proved his innocence "because he was already in custody." The greatest doubt cast on his guilt was that semen and pubic hair found on the victim's clothing was too little for positive DNA identification at the time of the trial.[10]

Six years later, however, DNA techniques had been improved enough to make such testing possible. McGinn's appeals attorney obtained a stay from a local judge so that the DNA testing might be done. A higher Texas state court overruled the judge and denied the appeal. Neither would the state board of pardons agree to hold up the execution while the testing was done. However, at the last minute, Texas Governor George W. Bush granted a stay of execution and ordered the DNA tests.[11]

They did not, however, prove McGinn's innocence. On the contrary, they established his guilt. He was executed by lethal injection on September 27, 2000.[12] For proponents of the death penalty, the McGinn case provides proof that the system functions properly.

How DNA Works

Just how well the establishing of guilt or innocence works in the future may to a large extent depend on DNA testing. DNA (deoxyribonucleic acid) is that part of the human chromosome that encodes genetic data. Each cell in a person's body, no matter where it is located, contains a tiny element called a double helix made up of strands of coiled units, which are unique to that person and that person alone. These strands are arranged in an order which is also unique to the individual. The DNA positively identifies the person. It is as specifically his or hers as are fingerprints.[13]

In murder cases, investigators collect biological material such as blood, hair, semen, or saliva from the crime scene and from the suspected killer. They mix these samples with chemicals which break down cellular material to extract the DNA molecules. The molecules are then treated with chemical primers, which produce longer fragments. Thirteen more primers multiply these strands into millions of distinctive molecules. These are treated with an electrical current, which sorts the molecules into thirteen color-coded bands imprinted on a gel.[14]

The crime scene samples are then compared with those taken from the suspect. According to scientists, "it's virtually impossible for unrelated people to match up perfectly on thirteen different levels. If samples do [match] odds that they're from one person are overwhelming."[15]

Since 1982, DNA evidence has established the innocence of more than seventy people convicted of crimes, "including eight on death row."[16] During that time, however, evidence which might have been suitable for DNA testing in many other cases has either not been tested, withheld from lawyers of the accused, not provided for death penalty appeals, or actually destroyed. In most cases this may have been a matter more of carelessness, or of misunderstanding the implications of the evidence, rather than of deliberate deceit. However, many death-row prisoners "have been denied the chance to prove their innocence using DNA technology that did not exist when they were convicted."[17]

No Needle for Miller

To ensure such omissions don't occur in the future, in February 2000, Democratic Senator Patrick Leahy of

Vermont sponsored the Innocence Protection Act in the Senate. In June of that year, a revised version of the bill was cosponsored by Republican Senator Gordon Smith of Oregon. It was designed to "prevent law enforcement officials from destroying DNA evidence," and to "allow prisoners on death row to request DNA testing on evidence that is in the government's possession."[18] It would "require the preservation of evidence after conviction" so that it would be available for death-row appeals.[19] As of this writing, the bill is still pending approval in both the House and Senate.

Meanwhile, such organizations as the Innocence Project of the Benjamin N. Cardozo School of Law in New York have zeroed in on DNA as perhaps the most important means there is of establishing innocence. The project has found that 23 percent of the convictions overturned by DNA testing were based on false confessions or admissions. Typical was the prosecution's videotaped "confession" by Robert Miller Jr., whose innocence was subsequently proved by DNA evidence. Once the DNA had done that, the appeals judge who viewed the videotape found that "there is nothing in these statements by the defendant which would in any way be considered a confession."[20]

Miller had been convicted and sentenced to death in Oklahoma in 1988 for raping and murdering ninety-two-year-old Zelma Cutler and 83-year-old Anna Laura Fowler. He was on death row for nine years following his conviction. For the last six of those years, "the state had DNA test results proving his innocence."[21]

The DNA evidence pointed to Ronald Lott, a man who pleaded guilty to raping two other elderly women. The same prosecutor was involved in both cases. At one point he told Miller's defense attorney, "We're gonna needle your client. You know, lethal injection, the needle."[22] DNA testing prevented that.

Hedging a Pardon

In an October 2000 case involving the Innocence Project, DNA evidence was used to secure a pardon in Virginia for a man who had been in prison for rape and murder for seventeen years. Earl Washington had been sentenced to death for the killing of Rebecca Williams. He was only a few days away from execution in 1994 when then-Governor L. Douglas Wilder reduced his sentence to life imprisonment. At that time, an initial DNA test "raised the possibility that someone else might have been involved" in the killing.[23]

It was six more years, however, before another Virginia governor, James S. Gilmore III, announced that a new DNA test "identified a known convicted rapist" other than Earl Washington to be "involved in the crime." The Innocence Project had brought pressure on Virginia authorities to conduct the second test. Now they protested when the governor insisted that Washington serve out a sentence for a separate and unrelated crime of which he was convicted. In the normal course of events, they pointed out, Washington would have been paroled for that crime eight years ago.[24]

"It is punitive, it is cruel, it is insensitive," charged codirector of the Innocence Project Barry C. Scheck. Governor Gilmore disagreed, pointing out through a spokesperson that the crime of which Washington was guilty had been particularly brutal. Washington, the spokesperson said, "is not a pillar of the community." The governor himself also refused to concede that Washington was innocent beyond doubt of the crime for which he had just pardoned him. "It is important for the public to understand," the governor stressed, "that absence of DNA evidence does not necessarily mean an individual is absent from the crime scene—just that he has not left any DNA markers." Innocence Project lawyers criticized the governor for not admitting that Washington "is stone cold innocent."[25]

The Debate Continues

According to an editorial in *The New York Times*, "modern DNA technology" has brought about "a dramatic shift in the nation's debate over capital punishment."[26] New organizations patterned after the Innocence Project have sprung up to push for more DNA testing in death penalty cases. Those who have fought against the death penalty for many years claim that present DNA findings exonerating prisoners on death row indicate that innocent people have been executed in the past for a variety of reasons that are ingrained in the death penalty system, and which DNA testing alone will not prevent. DNA material, they point out, is only available in a minority of homicide cases.

Those who favor capital punishment look at DNA differently. They see in its use an opportunity to do away with claims of wrongful executions. In a letter he wrote to *Newsweek* magazine, John Schank of San Pablo, California, summed up their argument: "With DNA testing helping to preclude the execution of innocent persons, it makes more sense than ever that criminals who kill someone in a brutal and heinous manner should forfeit their own lives."[27]

The debate over capital punishment will not end with DNA testing. Will justice be served more genuinely by it? That will depend on a host of other factors.

Six

THE JUSTICE SYSTEM
SYSTEM

All men are liable to error; and most men
are, in many points, by passion or
interest, under temptation to it.[1]
                    —Seventeenth century
        English philosopher John Locke

In the death penalty debate, the justice system itself is
an issue. So-called hanging judges, overly zealous
district attorneys, lazy or incompetent defense coun-
sels, biased juries, and politically appointed pardon and
parole boards all have been blamed for capital punishment injustices. They are charged with withholding and
distorting evidence, plea bargaining to elicit damaging
testimony, arousing emotions at the expense of truth,
and being more concerned with gaining political advan-
tage through death-row convictions than in seeking out
facts or mitigating circumstances. The result is a
system, according to death penalty opponents, in which
fatal miscarriages of justice are all too common.

If that accusation is true, however, it is also true that the system accurately reflects the will of the American people. For twenty-four years prior to 2000, not just polls, but the voting record of the public has affirmed overwhelming approval of the death penalty. Governors and mayors elected on law-and-order platforms have routinely appointed pro-death penalty judges. Other judges in favor of capital punishment have been elected directly by voters. These judges, however, didn't devise capital punishment; they have merely dispensed the justice that the people want.

The Hanging Judge

Have judges been too aggressive in death penalty cases? Opponents of the death penalty point to action taken by Florida Judge Robert McGregor in the case of Joseph "Crazy Joe" Spaziano as an example of judicial misconduct. Spaziano was convicted of the 1973 murder of eighteen-year-old Laura Lynn Harberts. The only witness against him was sixteen-year-old Tony DiLisio, who admittedly had a grudge against him because Spaziano had "been having a tumultuous affair with DiLisio's stepmother." At first DiLisio said he knew nothing about the murders. However, under hypnosis, he claimed to have been shown the victim's body, as well as the body of another victim, by Spaziano.[2]

Meanwhile, a lie detector test of another suspect, Lynwood Tate, "indicated strongly," according to police investigators, that he committed the murder. Tate, however, was never charged. Spaziano was, and he was convicted.[3]

The jury recommended "life imprisonment, rather than death." Judge Robert McGregor overruled the jury's instruction and sentenced Spaziano to die. According to University of Vermont law professor

Michael Mello, who worked on Spaziano's appeal, "it violated the federal constitution to override a jury recommendation of life imprisonment."[4]

Spaziano came "within inches of being executed" by the state of Florida. One day before the twentieth anniversary of his murder conviction, another judge ordered a new trial for him. That decision has been appealed to the Florida Supreme Court by the prosecution, and so Spaziano is still in prison. He is, however, no longer on death row where Judge McGregor's sentence had almost succeeded in having him executed.[5]

A Call for Impeachment

Advocates for the death penalty say that Judge McGregor's behavior was the exception, rather than the rule. They point out that the right of the judge to overrule a jury's sentence has been upheld by the United States Supreme Court. They insist that judicial misconduct cuts both ways. They point to Judge John T. Nixon of the Sixth U.S. District Court in Nashville, Tennessee, as an example. As part of his duties, Judge Nixon hears appeals in death penalty cases.[6]

Judge Nixon has decided five capital punishment cases "and has overturned all five of those lower-court convictions and sentences," according to his critics. In one of these cases, involving the confessed rapist and killer of an eight-year-old girl, Nixon had acted on the basis of "unconstitutionally vague definitions" given by the judge to the sentencing jury. Among the words which that judge used to characterize the crime were "heinous, atrocious and cruel." Eight previous courts who heard appeals in this case had refused to act. Only Nixon had done so.[7]

Judge John T. Nixon of the Sixth U.S. District Court in Nashville, Tennessee

His critics add that although Judge Nixon has never said he opposes the death penalty, "his *record* betrays him." They accuse him of delaying action on other death penalty cases for as long as ten years in order to effectively prevent executions from being carried out. They demand that Judge Nixon be impeached and removed from office.[8]

Pressure on Prosecutors

Pressure on judges perceived as reluctant to enforce the death penalty is not limited to Judge Nixon. In California, Texas, and Mississippi, coercion by their own party's governors and high party officials has in the past forced such judges out of office. Some of these judges were not against capital punishment. They just didn't act to impose it often enough to please the politicians whose power derived from its popularity. In Tennessee, Justice Penny White lost her seat on the state supreme court after the Republican Party mailed out a brochure reading: "Vote for Capital Punishment by Voting NO on August 1 for Supreme Court Justice Penny White." In Florida, Judge Steven W. Mansfield won office by pledging to punish defense attorneys who filed "frivolous appeals . . . in death penalty cases."[9]

The pressure is also brought to bear on those seeking such offices as district attorney, public prosecutor, or state attorney general. Once elected, they often pursue death penalty verdicts ferociously. "Trial and Error," a January 1999 nationwide study by the *Chicago Tribune*, "found 381 cases in which homicide convictions were set aside because prosecutors had failed to disclose evidence favorable to the defense or knowingly presented false evidence."[10]

Not a single one of the prosecutors involved was ever brought to trial for their actions in those cases.

Recently, however, three former prosecutors—Patrick King, Robert Kilander, and Thomas Knight—were indicted in DuPage County, Illinois, for engaging in an alleged "conspiracy to send a man to death row." The accused man involved was Rolando Cruz.[11]

Was Evidence Withheld?

Cruz, along with Alejandro Hernandez and Stephen Buckley, was accused of having participated in the rape and murder of ten-year-old Jeanine Nicarico. On February 25, 1983, Jeanine had stayed home from school with a cold. The front door of her house was kicked in and she was kidnapped. A clear boot print was visible on the door. Two days later Jeanine's body was found in a nearby woods.[12]

Thirteen months later Cruz, Hernandez, and Buckley were charged with the crime. Detectives said Cruz had described a vision to them of the murder, which coincided with the condition of the victim and the location where the body had been found. They also said that Hernandez told them that three people committed the crime and that two of the three were Buckley and somebody named "Ricky," not mentioning a last name. Jailhouse informants said Cruz had made statements incriminating himself. An expert found that the boot print left on the door matched Buckley's boots.[13]

A jury found Rolando Cruz and Hernandez guilty. However, they deadlocked on Buckley, and in his case a mistrial was declared. Cruz and Hernandez were sentenced to death. Their convictions were set aside in 1988 when the Illinois Supreme Court ruled that they should have been tried separately. It was 1990 when Cruz went on trial for a second time. He was again convicted and sentenced to death. Tried separately, Hernandez was convicted and sentenced to eighty years in prison. Both their convictions were subsequently reversed on the grounds that the jury had not heard certain evidence.[14]

In 1995, Rolando Cruz went on trial for the third time. This trial was different. Cruz had always denied that he had told detectives of having a vision of the murder scene, and now testimony by one of them indicated that the story might have been cooked up by the investigators, and that the prosecutors knew this. Hernandez repeated his insistence that what he had told detectives about the crime was a stupid self-incriminating lie cooked up in hopes of collecting a $10,000 reward for information leading to the capture of the killers. The jailhouse informants who testified that Cruz had told them things that tied him to the crime now took back their testimony. It was brought out that the boot print identification had been denied by the Illinois State Police crime lab, the FBI crime lab, and one other expert, and that a second expert who testified to the match had originally identified a print taken from the ground outside the door as that of a woman's shoe too small to match the boots worn by Buckley. Evidence was presented that Brian Dugan, who had confessed to two other murders, including that of a seven-year-old girl, had admitted to killing Jeanine Nicarico. All this data had been withheld from the defense by prosecutors.[15]

Only A Few Bad Apples

This time Rolando Cruz was found not guilty. After twelve years in jail, much of the time on death row, he was a free man. Shortly after his release, a special prosecutor was appointed to investigate the handling of his case. The result was the charges brought against Patrick King, Robert Kilander, and Thomas Knight—the three

Rolando Cruz, right, stands with his attorney during a presentation to college students a week after he was acquitted of the murder of Jeanine Nicarico.

prosecutors involved—as well as against four sheriff's investigators.[16] The prosecutors, however, were ultimately acquitted.

Following the Cruz case, there were other investigations. Prosecutorial misconduct in additional cases was unearthed. However, the 381 cases documented by the *Chicago Tribune* represent a tiny percentage of the thousands of murder trials conducted in the United States every year. According to John Justice, president of the National District Attorneys Association, "the great majority of prosecutors in this country are truly dedicated to doing their jobs in the proper fashion."[17]

There seems little reason to doubt that. Nor is there reason to believe that most defense attorneys in capital cases fall short of exerting their best efforts in representing their clients. The few who do, however, offer a horrifying picture of how the justice system can fail a poor defendant. The most well-known example of this is Ronald G. Mock, the defense attorney for Gary Graham, the condemned man whose ordeal and execution are described in Chapter One.

The "Mock Wing"

Mock had been appointed to defend Graham in Harris County, which like most counties in Texas doesn't have a public-defender system. Elected judges appoint counsel for defendants too poor to hire a lawyer. At the time of Graham's trial, "judges routinely appointed lawyers who moved cases quickly." Often, according to *The New York Times*, "there was pressure on lawyers to contribute to the judges' campaigns." Mock was a favorite of the judges both before and after Graham's trial. During the 1980s he estimates that he made

Was Gary Graham, pictured here two weeks before his execution, the victim of a substandard defense? If he could have afforded better counsel, would he be alive today?

between $120,000 and $130,000 a year defending homicide cases.[18]

He lost twelve of those cases. Seven of the men he defended, including Graham, had already been executed by July 2000. Five were awaiting execution. Death row at the Texas state prison in Livingston is referred to by inmates and their lawyers as "the Mock Wing." Five of Mock's death-row clients filed for appeals, which accused him of "ineffectiveness of counsel."[19]

Mock shrugs this off. He boasts that "he has had more clients sentenced to death than any lawyer in the country." He admits that he flunked criminal law at Texas Southern University. He concedes that "I drank a lot of whiskey," but insists that "it never affected my performance." The Texas Bar Association disagrees. It has reprimanded Mock repeatedly for professional misconduct.[20]

Do Fees Affect Justice?

Attorney Mock does have some defenders. Judge Richard Trevathan has said that "I always thought Ron Mock was a good lawyer." Harris County assistant district attorney Roe Wilson believes "Ron did a competent job" handling the Graham case. Wilson also reminds us that "by law you are not guaranteed perfect or excellent counsel. You're guaranteed competent counsel."[21]

"Competent counsel," however, may too often be a standard defined by where the trial takes place. New York, New Jersey, and Colorado, for example, have "multimillion-dollar capital defender offices that provide teams of lawyers and investigators for people in death penalty trials."[22] This has led to the New York State District Attorney's Association setting up a "mutual help policy" in which better-financed prosecutors from large cities provide help in death penalty cases to rural prosecutors in counties with limited resources. The death penalty is relatively new in New York and the fear is that unfavorable outcomes by underfinanced prosecutions might result in judicial rulings that "could set precedents that would hurt prosecutors across the state."[23]

This is not the case in most states where, according to opponents of the death penalty, capital cases are heavily weighted against defendants. While some states have public defenders for capital offenders, others appoint defense lawyers and too often underpay them and are stingy with the funds necessary to mount a proper defense. Texas, Virginia, Georgia, and Mississippi offer extremely low payment to defense lawyers. Mississippi pays a flat fee of $1,000 plus costs for death penalty cases. Alabama, "with a death row growing at the fastest rate in the country," pays defense attorneys in capital cases so little that many lawyers turn down the work.[24]

Birmingham, Alabama, lawyer Wilson Meyers didn't turn down a capital case, and when it was over, he billed the court $13,399 for conducting the defense. The judge said that was "too excessive," and reduced the payment to $4,128. When his investigator and paralegal helper were paid, Meyers was left with $1,212, which he says came to about $5.05 an hour. Meyers says he won't be taking any more murder cases. "I do not have the financial resources to absorb a cut of that amount," he says.[25]

Are Penalty Hearings Unfair?

In most death penalty cases there are two phases. The first is a trial to determine the defendant's innocence or guilt. The second is to determine what his or her sentence should be.

The second hearing may involve friends, family, clergy, or employers of the convicted person testifying as to good character, childhood abuse, extraordinary pressures, or other factors known as mitigating circumstances. These are intended to humanize the person and to make the crime seem less terrible, and perhaps even somewhat understandable. On the other side, survivors of the victim or victims are also allowed to testify in many cases where the death penalty is an option. Usually their testimony is emotional, possibly vengeful, and often survivor witnesses insist on closure through execution.

In the Alabama case of convicted murderer Robert Lee Tarver Jr., his attorney offered no evidence of his drinking problem and strong family ties during the sentencing phase of the trial. The judge who sentenced Tarver to death later said he would have been more lenient had he known such things about Tarver. Anti-capital punishment groups fear that the emotional impact of survivor testimony, particularly when not balanced by testimony favorable to the convicted criminal, puts an unfair burden on the defense during the penalty phase of the trial. In Alabama they found that "court-appointed lawyers spent an average of three hours trying the penalty phase."[26] Those against the death penalty say that this is far too little time to make an effective case for leniency.

Guilt and Innocence

Improper defense, during both trial and sentencing hearings, is the factor most often cited as the reason for setting aside the death penalty during the appeals process. Many convictions have been reversed because of court-appointed defense lawyers who came to trial drunk, fell asleep during testimony, made no effort to uncover evidence or witnesses proving their client's innocence, or failed to present mitigating circumstances during sentencing hearings. It is becoming more difficult, however, to reverse the effects of such behavior through the appeals process.

In an article by Susan Blaustein, the *Nation* reported that "the Supreme Court has issued more than a dozen rulings that have severely limited the number and scope" of appeals that may work their way up through state courts to the federal court system.[27] Other journalists have noted that "the court held that a death-row inmate who presents only newly discovered evidence of innocence is generally not entitled to a hearing in federal court. The court implied that it is not a constitutional violation to execute an individual who may be entirely innocent."[28]

It is not only questions of absolute innocence or absolute guilt that fuel the death penalty debate. It is the relative nature of guilt and innocence, the intent behind the capital crime, the degree of premeditation, the emotional state of the killer, the circumstances. Is the battered wife who shoots her husband as deserving of the death penalty as the serial killer? Should society execute the betrayed lover maddened by jealousy alongside the hit man? Is the thief who shoots a police officer in self-defense as deserving of a death sentence as the one who deliberately plans to murder the payroll guard in order to get at the money? These are the questions that sentencing juries and sentencing judges must decide.

Are Capital Juries Biased?

Of the thirty-eight states that have capital punishment, in only five—Arizona, Colorado, Idaho, Montana, and

Nebraska—do judges act alone in deciding the death penalty. In four other states—Alabama, Florida, Delaware, and Indiana—judges may override a jury's sentencing decision. (Death penalty opponents question the constitutionality of this.) In other states, juries must not only decide whether the defendant is guilty, but also whether the death penalty should be imposed.[29]

From the first, there has been controversy over death penalty opponents sitting on murder juries. In theory, someone who is against the death penalty cannot legally be barred from serving. However, the person must be able to state that he or she would be able to impose the fatal sentence if the case merited it. In practice, prosecutors and/or judges often find reasons to exclude those against capital punishment from juries.[30]

Those who favor capital punishment claim it is only common sense to bar death penalty opponents from juries that may decide to execute convicted murderers. Those against capital punishment believe that this stacks juries in favor of recommending death over life imprisonment. A 1997 study by the National Science Foundation found that many of those who served on death penalty juries "misunderstood what it means to find a defendant worthy of the death penalty 'beyond a reasonable doubt.'"[31]

The Key Question

These are only some of the many questions which ask not whether the death penalty is right or wrong, but rather whether it is or can be applied fairly. In Illinois, when Governor Ryan suspended executions, it was because of the fear of killing innocent persons. Justice For All (JFA), a pro-death penalty organization, claims "there is no evidence that an innocent person has ever been executed in Illinois."[32]

They remind us that nationwide "the actual imposition of the death penalty is rare." Even among those serving death sentences, including some who have been on death row for a decade or more, only one-fifth of one percent are actually executed each year. The rest benefit from a justice system that is designed to give them every benefit of every doubt before their sentences are carried out.[33]

Admittedly, that system isn't perfect. Like every system it has its flaws. In the end we come back to the original question: Does the capital punishment justice system really serve the public interest?

Seven

TOO YOUNG TO DIE?

I *smiled at Mr. Grunow and he smiled at me. He pushed the gun away like he thought it was fake. It was kind of like a joke—the kind of joke we always had between us. Then the gun went off. I don't know how it happened.*"[1]

—Thirteen-year-old Nathaniel Brazill,
explaining how he shot and killed his
English teacher, Barry Grunow

Between 1976 when the death penalty was reinstituted, and January 2001, 683 men and women were put to death in the United States. Thirteen were convicted murderers who had been under the age of eighteen when they committed their crimes. At the beginning of 2001, there were 3,726 people on death rows in the United States. As of August 2000, 80 of them were youthful offenders awaiting execution.[2]

The Child Welfare League of America, the National Parents and Teachers Association, the National Council on Crime and Delinquency, the American Ortho-psychiatric Association, and many other organizations have come out against capital punishment for minors. The American Bar Association opposes death sentences for "any person for an offense committed while under the age of eighteen." Amnesty International bases its objection "on recognition that minors are not fully mature—hence not fully responsible."[3]

Dianne Clements, president of Justice For All, disagrees. "The individuals are not juveniles," she says. "The fact that these people are called juveniles . . . is nothing more than an attempt to create an environment that makes these people appear sympathetic, so [the public] will envision some innocent, sweet young child who is being executed—not the capital murderer who is being executed."[4] Columnist James J. Kilpatrick points to the crime committed by sixteen-year-old Heath Wilkins, who brutally raped and killed his victim, and after describing the crime to authorities, "started laughing." Kilpatrick points out that the United States Supreme Court has held that the execution of murderers who committed their crimes as juveniles is constitutional.[5]

In cases of particularly horrendous crimes, the judge may decide to try the juvenile as an adult. In such cases the accused may be charged with first-degree murder and may face the death penalty. However, United States Supreme Court decisions, and in many cases state laws, forbid the execution of persons who were under the age of sixteen at the time the crime was committed, even though they may have been tried and convicted as an adult. Actually, minors—those under the age of eighteen—are rarely executed before their eighteenth birthday. For this reason, the discussion involving the punishment of minors who commit capital crimes really boils down to whether those who commit them between the ages of sixteen and eighteen should be executed after they become adults. At present, such executions are constitutional.

The Myth of the "Superpredator"

Constitutional or not, the practice sets the United States apart from other countries. The United Nations Convention on the Rights of the Child forbids putting to death those who committed their crimes under age eighteen. Only two nations have not ratified the document: Somalia and the United States. Also, while the United States is one of the more than one hundred forty-four countries that signed the International Covenant on Civil and Political Rights, it specifically reserved its right to ignore the covenant's ban on the executions of minors.[6]

Why does the United States take such a hard line toward young killers in contrast to other countries? The attitude can be traced back to the late 1960s when the war on drugs began. At that time there were no executions in the United States. However, as drug-related violence grew despite the war on drugs, public attitudes toward offenders hardened. Many of these offenders were inner-city youth gang members recruited by drug dealers to battle other dealers for larger shares of the growing illegal crack cocaine market. By the late 1980s and early 1990s, there was a considerable increase in the number of juveniles charged with murder.

By the end of 1995 there was mounting public concern that youth violence was out of control, and that the number of murders committed by young people was growing at an alarming rate. Pointing out that the juvenile population was increasing, Professor John DiJulio of Princeton saw a threat that "remorseless and morally impoverished" youths would overrun the nation's streets. A new kind of adolescent had developed, one Professor DiJulio dubbed a "superpredator."[7]

Actually, the growth in crimes of violence by juveniles had peaked by that time and was already starting to decrease. By 2000, despite the growth in the adolescent population, juvenile crime had been declining in the United States for seven straight years. Nevertheless, press coverage of violent murders by minors continues to convince the public that young people today are more murderous than ever. One result of this is that "twenty-three states now have no bottom age limit for kids to be tried as adults."[8]

Not Too Young to Kill

California does have such a limit. In that state children under the age of fourteen cannot be charged with murder. That is fortunate for the killers of three-year-old Damien Stiffler. His sister and her friend, who committed the crime in August 2000, were six years old and five years old respectively. They confessed to Sergeant Mark Lohman of the Riverside County Sheriff's Department. He says they did it deliberately. "They meant to kill Damien by suffocating him with a pillow."[9]

Although it is impossible that the two little girls could face the death penalty in any state, some people believe that should be changed. One of the controversies surrounding capital punishment is just how old people who kill should be before they pay the ultimate penalty for their crime. Some people do not believe that teen killers should be exempted from execution.

One such person is Brett Blackwell, an advocate of the Bill of Rights and a member of the National Rifle Association. He was outraged by demonstrations against thirteen-year-old honor student Nathaniel Brazill being tried as an adult for the murder of his English teacher, Barry Grunow. The day of the murder, Brazill had been suspended from the Lake Worth Community Middle School in Florida for throwing water balloons. He went home and then returned to school with a loaded gun. It was the last hour on the last day of school—May 26, 2000. Nathaniel went to Grunow's classroom to talk to a girl he had a crush on. When Grunow denied him permission to talk to the girl, Brazill took out the gun. An instant later Grunow was dead. Brazill said he didn't mean to pull the trigger.[10]

Brett Blackwell expresses doubt that the gun "viciously emerged from his pocket, unaided by Brazill, and accidentally went off and shot the teacher with pinpoint accuracy." He points out that "my children know the difference between right and wrong, but apparently Brazill doesn't." Blackwell concludes that "I would welcome the death penalty in this matter."[11]

Jonesboro and Columbine

Many people would not agree with Blackwell. At the same time, public concern over murders committed by young people has been rearoused since March 1998 by two high-profile school yard massacres, and by the violent incidents involving youths, which followed them. The fact that the slaughters at Westside Middle School in Jonesboro, Arkansas, and Columbine High School in Littleton, Colorado, did not take place in poor neighborhoods or urban areas, seemed a wake-up call. Small towns and suburbs were suddenly faced with the fact that youngsters from middle-class homes were capable of killing sprees.

Left: Mitchell Johnson, pictured in 1997.
Right: Andrew Golden, pictured in 1996

The first incident, in Jonesboro, occurred on March 27, 1998. Thirteen-year-old Mitchell Johnson and eleven-year-old Andrew Golden, Johnson's cousin, set off a fire alarm at the Westside Middle School. Then, dressed in camouflage, they hid in the woods overlooking the school grounds and fired a volley of bullets and shotgun shells into the groups of students and teachers exiting the school. One teacher and four students under the age of thirteen were killed. Eleven other people were wounded. The adult world was shocked. A contributor to *The South End*, a newsmagazine Web site, called for "the death penalty . . . for such a dastardly transgression." Others agreed with him. The maximum sentence under Arkansas law, however, was confinement to a juvenile facility until the age of twenty-one, and that's what the judge decreed for the two boys.[12]

A year later, in Littleton, Colorado, on the morning of April 21, 1999, two Columbine High School students armed with guns and bombs opened fire and murdered thirteen people and wounded twenty-eight others. The killers were eighteen-year-old Eric Harris, and seventeen-year-old Dylan Klebold. They were members of a group of adolescent males who called themselves the Trench Coat Mafia and decorated their black coats with swastikas. The day of the massacre was the 110th anniversary of Adolf Hitler's birth.[13]

"I saw them shoot a girl because she was praying to God," said fifteen-year-old survivor Evan Todd. "They shot a black kid. They called him a nigger. They said they didn't like niggers, so they shot him in the face."[14]

The Pressures of Adolescence

The slaughter came to an end only when Harris and Klebold shot and killed themselves. A question remained. It was the same heart-wrenching question that was asked following the Jonesboro massacre: Why? Why would young people commit such horrible acts?

Psychiatrists and psychologists say that the time between childhood and adulthood is a period of emotional, as well as mental and physical, change and growth. These are the years when young people are establishing their identities. They are developing decision-making abilities, judgment, and impulse control. This is, perhaps, the most difficult time of anyone's life. Self-doubt is common, and self-confidence is shaky. This is true for all developing adults, but it is particularly true for those who are drawn to violence, including those who kill. In addition, according to the American Society for Adolescent Psychiatry, adolescents who murder "very often suffer from serious psychological and family disturbances," which make the normal doubts and pressures of adolescence much worse.[15]

Capital punishment opponents believe this is a reason why both the young and the mentally incompetent should be spared the death penalty. This view includes both convicted killers who are insane, and those who are retarded. Twenty-five states permit the execution of retarded murderers. According to the United States Supreme Court, "executing . . . the insane violates the Constitution's Eighth Amendment," but that ruling does not include the mentally retarded.[16]

Even Brothers Disagree

That omission was key to the controversy surrounding the execution in Texas of Oliver David Cruz on August 9, 2000. Cruz had "an IQ of either 64 or 76, depending on the test." At his trial a defense psychologist testified that Cruz was "mentally retarded." The prosecutor didn't deny this, but insisted that because Cruz "may not be very smart," he was "more dangerous," and therefore should be put to death.[17]

In 1988, Oliver Cruz and Jerry Kemplin had approached twenty-four-year-old air force technician Kelly Elizabeth Donovan as she was taking a walk on a street in San Antonio, Texas. They seized the young woman and abducted her. Cruz raped her and then stabbed her twenty times, killing her. The police arrested the two men soon after the murder. Jerry Kemplin testified against Cruz in a plea bargaining deal, which gained him a prison term rather than a death sentence. Cruz confessed to the crime. "She was just someone," was how he explained choosing Kelly Elizabeth Donovan to be his victim.[18]

Prior to his execution, there was an organized campaign to save Cruz. It was based on his being retarded. An editorial in *The New York Times* maintained that "executing the mentally retarded offends the most basic standards of justice."[19] John Derbyshire of the *National Review*, writing after Cruz had been executed, saw it differently. He wrote: "I cannot see why a person who has functioned in the world should be spared any penalty that the law considers proper." He went on to point out that "Oliver Cruz took the life of Kelly Donovan, knowing what he was doing. He has paid with his own life. We do not exult or gloat, but we can, without guilt or shame, feel a grim satisfaction in wrong redressed, in justice accomplished."[20]

When it comes to executing mental incompetents, or children, for that matter, there is not just disagreement between pro- and anti-death penalty advocates. There are differences among those who favor capital punishment as well. Both George W. Bush and his brother, Governor Jeb Bush of Florida, are strong supporters of the death penalty. As governor of Texas,

George W. Bush opposed laws that would ban the execution of the mentally retarded. Governor Jeb Bush, however, has said that "people with clear mental retardation should not be executed."[21]

To successfully plead insanity in a murder case, a defendant must prove that he or she does not know right from wrong. Those who think that the mentally retarded should not be executed would lower that standard to spare those who are retarded and therefore incapable of making reasonable adult judgments. It is a standard that already applies to children in most states. However, those who oppose lowering the standard for the mentally retarded think it amounts to making lower intelligence a license to kill.

Eight

IS CAPITAL PUNISHMENT BIASED?

The denizens of death row are black as molasses, and the staff are white bread.[1]
—Pennsylvania death-row
inmate Mumia Abu-Jamal

At the end of May 2000, "the most recognizable death-row inmate in the land," according to *The New York Times*, was Mumia Abu-Jamal. A civil rights activist who became a prominent black radio journalist in Philadelphia, Abu-Jamal had never been arrested before being charged with murder in December 1981. He had, however, gained national prominence by his strong and repeated charges of racism against the Philadelphia police.[2]

By October 2000, Abu-Jamal had been on death row for eighteen years. He was waiting for a hearing which would determine whether he would be set free, granted a new trial, or executed. Briefs supporting his appeal for this hearing had been submitted by the American Civil Liberties Union, the National Association for the

Advancement of Colored People (NAACP), the National Lawyers Guild, and other national legal organizations, as well as by twenty-two members of the British Parliament and the Chicana/Chicano Studies Foundation. Petitions to set aside his sentence and pleas on his behalf from prominent people had come from all over the world. In Paris and other European cities, thousands marched to protest against the state of Pennsylvania executing him. The main criticism of his conviction is that it was the result of bias against Abu-Jamal because he is a black man.[3]

The Case of Mumia Abu-Jamal

Police and prosecutors involved in the case deny any bias. They say that on the night of December 9, 1981, Philadelphia police officer Daniel Faulkner made a routine traffic stop of a car being driven by Abu-Jamal's brother. They say that Abu-Jamal arrived on the scene while the officer was arguing with his brother. According to the authorities, Abu-Jamal shot Officer Faulkner in the back. Faulkner returned the fire, hitting Abu-Jamal, and then Abu-Jamal stood over the policeman and shot him in the head, killing him.[4]

The police say they found Abu-Jamal's gun nearby. Five bullets had been fired from it. A witness identified Abu-Jamal as the shooter. Three other witnesses, two of them police officers, testified that they had heard Abu-Jamal boast about the killing at Thomas Jefferson University Hospital while awaiting treatment for his wounds. After Abu-Jamal was convicted, it took the jury less than four hours to sentence him to death.[5]

Abu-Jamal's supporters challenge the police account. They say it was not Abu-Jamal, but someone else who shot Officer Faulkner. They say the bullet

Supporters of Mumia Abu-Jamal claim that racial bias has overridden justice in his death penalty sentence.

removed from Faulkner's brain was a .44 caliber, while the gun Abu-Jamal was charged with having fired was a .38. Nor were Abu-Jamal's fingerprints found on the gun.[6]

Those who champion his cause point out that the only witness who took the stand against Abu-Jamal was a prostitute, Cynthia White. They claim that two other prostitutes, Veronica Jones and Pamela Jenkins, were told by authorities that if they testified against Abu-Jamal, they could continue to practice their profession without being arrested. Abu-Jamal's defenders also point out that Robert Chobert, a white cab driver who was a witness to the shooting, told police that the shooter was a 225-pound man who "ran away" from the scene of the crime, and that four other witnesses also said they saw another man fleeing after the shooting. As for the testimony of Abu-Jamal's having boasted of committing the crime while in the hospital, the officers who say they heard this never mentioned having done so until two months after his arrest.[7]

The Philadelphia Story

At the very least, say his supporters, there is reasonable doubt as to Mumia Abu-Jamal's guilt. They point to the record of Judge Albert Sabo, who presided over Abu-Jamal's trial, conviction, and sentencing. Judge Sabo "has sentenced thirty-two people to death—more than twice the number of people than any other judge in the country. All but two were people of color."[8]

It was Abu-Jamal's bad luck, say death penalty opponents, to have to seek justice in Philadelphia. Lynne Abraham, the city's district attorney, has been labeled "The Deadliest D.A." in the United States by the media. A training video for new Philadelphia prosecutors advised that "blacks from low-income areas" should be excluded from juries because they "are less likely to convict." More than half the death sentences handed down in Pennsylvania are from Philadelphia, which has only 14 percent of the state's population. Eighty-three percent of those on death row from Philadelphia are African American. A 1998 study revealed that the odds of being sentenced to death in Philadelphia are approximately 3.9 times greater for black defendants than for whites.[9]

The key factor in biased death sentencing, however, is not the race of the defendant, but rather the race of the victim. In Florida, Illinois, Oklahoma, North Carolina, and Mississippi, for instance, a death sentence is four to five and a half times more likely to be decreed "if the victim was white than if the victim was black," according to a 1998 report by the Death Penalty Information Center. The report further stated that "in 96 percent of the studies examining the relationship between race and the death penalty there was a pattern of . . . discrimination."[10]

Other Factors

According to the Death Penalty Information Center, "half of those on death row are from minority populations that make up only 20 percent of the country's population. Blacks are represented on death row at three and a half times their proportion in the population as a whole."[11] However, some social scientists argue that racial discrimination is not responsible for the sentencing to death of such high numbers of blacks as compared to whites. They say that there are other factors, often not taken into consideration, which account for the disparity.

For instance, they dispute the idea of death penalty prejudice based on the race of the victim. They say that more African Americans receive the death penalty for killing whites than for killing blacks because there are far more whites in the population. They point out that most same-race homicides occur between people who know each other. They are the result of family quarrels or crimes of passion—unpremeditated killings which are not capital crimes and don't usually result in first-degree murder charges leading to the death penalty.

On the other hand, blacks who kill whites usually do so during the course of a crime such as armed robbery or rape, committed against a stranger. This may mean the difference between being charged with second-degree murder, for which there is no death penalty, or murder in the first degree, a capital crime, for which there is. Also, more blacks than whites are repeat offenders, and therefore more likely to receive more severe sentences, including the death penalty.

A 1991 Rand Corporation study that is often quoted by death penalty proponents found that "white murderers received the death penalty slightly more often (32 percent) than nonwhite murderers (27 percent)." A study of the death penalty system in the United States by Patrick A. Lanagan, senior statistician at the Department of Justice Bureau of Justice Statistics, did not "find evidence that the justice system is treating blacks and whites differently."[12] Stanley Rothman and Stephen Powers, director and research assistant at the Center for the Study of Social and Political Change at Smith College, concluded that "while there is justification for the claim that discriminatory capital sentencing occurred in the past, the charge that they persist today lacks support."[13]

African American Attitudes

Opinion in the African-American community is divided about the involvement of bias in capital punishment. "Mistrust of the criminal justice system, and a disproportionate number of African Americans behind bars," according to University of Chicago sociologist Robert Sampson, "are the reasons many blacks say they oppose the death penalty." However, that began to change in the last years of the twentieth century. Only 40 percent of American blacks were for the death penalty in 1974, but a survey by the National Opinion Research Center at the University of Chicago found that the percentage had grown to 57 percent by 1996.[14]

Today the focus of many African Americans is on drive-by shootings and other impersonal violence. Like whites, they are appalled by such brutality. Although violent crime is decreasing, the perception of both whites and blacks is that the streets of America are dangerous and too many people are being caught in the criminal crossfire. This is particularly true in inner-city areas where many innocent victims are black.

"When you commit a murder and you know what's going to happen when you get caught, then it might make some people think twice," says thirty-two-year-old Darryl Clay, a Detroit black man who favors capital punishment. At age seventy-eight, African American Anna Jones declares that "I'd be certainly willing to see the death penalty here in Michigan," a state that does not have capital punishment.[15]

Is Prejudice Built into the System?

These views do not agree with those of African-American leaders. The NAACP strongly opposes capital punishment, as does the Southern Christian Leadership Council (SCLC) and the Urban League. Influential black leaders like former South African President Nelson Mandela, Reverend Jesse Jackson, authors John Edgar Wideman and Ernest J. Gaines, civil rights activist Coretta Scott King, and others have spoken out against the death penalty.

In general, their opposition is based on what they consider to be the immorality of the state killing individuals. However, there is also a strong feeling among black leaders that the system is set up in a way that is biased against minorities. Reverend Jesse Jackson points out that "there are no objective rules or guidelines for when a prosecutor should seek the death penalty, when a jury should recommend it, and when a judge should give it." He says that this "ensures that the application of the death penalty will be discriminatory against racial, gender, and ethnic groups."[16]

In almost all jurisdictions that have capital punishment, the prosecutor is the one who decides whether or not to seek the death penalty. A 1998 study by Professor Jeffrey Pokorak of St. Mary's University School of Law revealed that "only 1 percent of the district attorneys in death penalty states in this country are black and only 1 percent are Hispanic. The remaining 97.5 percent are white."[17] To many black leaders, this indicates that black lives risk being at the mercy of white prejudices.

In September 2000, a Justice Department review of the administration of the federal death penalty showed that it too was subject to "significant racial . . . disparities." More than half of the cases in which a federal prosecutor sought a sentence of death involved an African-American defendant. The death penalty for federal crimes has been law since 1988, but as of this writing no one has actually been executed. Nevertheless, African-American leaders are disturbed at the number of death sentences imposed on black defendants considering that blacks are only 12 percent of the population of the United States.[18]

Federal and state bias against blacks in death penalty sentencing must be viewed as part of the larger problem of racial discrimination in the United States. Its existence can't be denied. When its focus zeroes in on matters of life and death, however, both sides of the capital punishment controversy recognize that prejudice must not be allowed to prevail.

Nine

CARRYING OUT THE SENTENCE

The executioner's face is always well hidden . . .[1]
—From "A Hard Rain's A-Gonna Fall"
by Bob Dylan

Fred Leuchter is not exactly an executioner. He is, however, as he himself puts it, "in the execution field." He calls himself an "execution technologist." He is a specialist in execution hardware.[2]

At the start of his career, his specialty was building and repairing electric chairs. Soon his expertise extended to hangmen's equipment and gallows. Then, moving right along with modern technology, Leuchter started designing lethal injection devices. One of his most recent clients was the state of New Jersey.[3]

In keeping with his profession, Leuchter is strongly pro-death penalty. At the same time, he believes that convicted murderers have the right to die with dignity and without suffering. Toward this end, he strives to design new equipment that is "more humane." He takes pride in his work. "I sleep well at night," says Leuchter, because "people executed by my machines have dignified, painless deaths."[4]

The Blade That Failed

Throughout most of history, painless deaths were not the goal of death sentences. Suffering was a deliberate part of the process prior to the nineteenth century. Executions were public exhibitions meant to impress potential criminals with the pain of fatal punishment. In ancient Rome and Japan, criminals were nailed to crosses and left to die slowly in plain view of those passing by. Culprits in Rome might also be fed alive to wild animals. In South America and Africa the condemned were carved up slowly. In Europe during the Middle Ages, they were pulled apart by horses, or burned alive.

Toward the end of the eighteenth century, beheading by an ax-wielding executioner was a preferred means of carrying out sentences of death in Europe. Too often the axman's aim was off and the execution was botched. The culprit would suffer horribly and in extreme cases might end up being hacked to death.

Such exhibitions appalled a French physician named Joseph-Ignace Guillotin. Like Fred Leuchter many years later, Dr. Guillotin thought that even the worst of criminals was entitled to a quick and painless death. In 1792, he developed a machine intended to accomplish that. It was called the guillotine.[5]

It involved a heavily weighted blade being dropped between two grooved posts and a board at the bottom, which was molded to hold the head of the victim firmly in place. Unfortunately, over the long run the guillotine did not fulfill its humane goal. The grooves in the posts

This drawing demonstrates the use of the guillo-tine in late eighteenth-century France.

became worn with use so that the blade wobbled as it came down and struck its target. Too often the person being executed was not positioned correctly and the head was not severed. The results were gruesome and horrible, which may explain why this method was never used in the United States.[6]

The Electric Chair

A toy guillotine, a favorite with French children, did, however, become popular in the United States. It was a forerunner of Death Row Marv, a battery-operated robot-type toy, which is presently being "marketed for ages thirteen and up" and sells "for about $20." Death Row Marv is seated in an electric chair. Young customers are advised to "watch Marv convulse as the switch is thrown." His eyes "glow red as he fries."[7]

This is in contrast to the original purpose of the life-size electric chair. When its use was first proposed in 1881, the United States Supreme Court declared that it would "produce instantaneous and therefore painless death."[8] It was used for the first time at Auburn State Prison in New York. However, despite the efforts of Fred Leuchter and others, there have been many botched electrocutions. One of the most horrifying was that of Pedro Medina in Florida on March 25, 1997. Witnesses described how "flames up to a foot long shot out from the right side of Medina's head" and said there was "the smell of burnt flesh."[9]

As of November 2000, there had been 149 executions by electrocution since the reintroduction of the death penalty in 1976. Florida had recently switched from electrocution to lethal injection, and the electric chair was still being used in only ten states—Alabama, Arkansas, Georgia, Kentucky, Nebraska, Ohio, Oklahoma,

The electric chair at the Louisiana State Penitentiary at Angola . . .

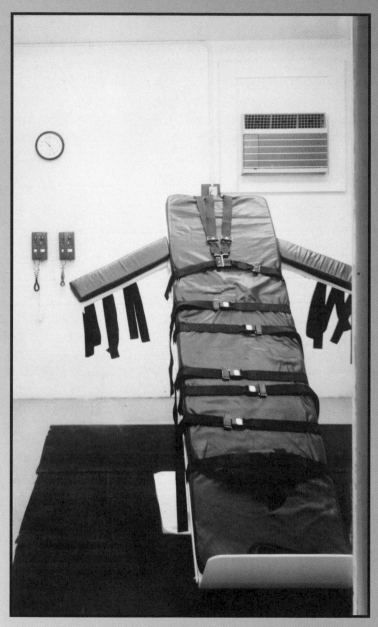

*. . . and the lethal injection chamber
at the same prison.*

South Carolina, Tennessee, and Virginia. In eight of the ten, lethal injection was offered as an alternative method of carrying out the death penalty. Other methods of execution still in use in the United States include the gas chamber (still used in five states with lethal injection as an alternative), hanging (two states, both offering a choice of lethal injection), and the firing squad (two states which also offer lethal injection).[10]

Lethal Injection

Lethal injection has become the preferred means of execution because other techniques proved messy and sometimes agonizing. Hanging is considered "a painful and inhumane method of execution," even by many of those who favor the death penalty, because of cases in which the condemned person's neck did not break and he or she slowly strangled to death. In the gas chamber many of the condemned have tried to hold their breath, a reaction that produces convulsions and prolongs the agony of dying for as long as fifteen minutes. Firing squads have too often proved inaccurate, painfully wounding before finally killing their target.[11]

Recent cases suggest that lethal injection also may not live up to its claims of providing a clean and painless death. To receive a lethal injection, the inmate is first strapped to a gurney by the ankles and wrists. Three tubes are inserted into three separate veins. "A deadly quantity of three different drugs" is injected directly into the bloodstream through the tubes. The first drug is sodium thiopental, a dose large enough to make the subject lose consciousness. The second is pancuronium bromide "which paralyzes the lungs and diaphragm, causing the inmate to stop breathing." Finally, potassium chloride is administered. That stops the heart.[12]

A problem with this is that not all people react to the same doses of this combination of drugs in the same way. Asthmatics may present one set of problems, diabetics another, and so forth. Allergies may present difficulties. In particular, a history of drug use—which many of those on death row have—complicates the insertion of the tubes into the veins and stretches out the process, causing both physical and psychological pain. The U.S. Court of Appeals has observed that there is evidence that "lethal injection poses a serious risk of cruel, protracted death," adding that "even a slight error in dosage or administration can leave a prisoner conscious but paralyzed while dying, a . . . witness of his or her own asphyxiation."[13]

The Torment of Bennie Demps

The execution of Bennie Demps in Florida on June 7, 2000, is an example of the difficulties with lethal injection. As described in Chapter Three, Demps had been convicted of murdering two people and then, while in prison, of holding down another inmate while someone else stabbed him. He claimed he had been framed in the second case because he had been spared the death penalty in the earlier one.[14]

"They butchered me back there!" Demps told those who had come to witness his execution as he was wheeled into the death chamber on the gurney. He said he had been strapped to the gurney for thirty-three minutes while technicians "struggled to insert the lethal intravenous drip into a vein." He told the witnesses that "I was in a lot of pain. They cut me in the groin; they cut me in the leg; I was bleeding profusely."[15]

Authorities said Demps had been "strapped to the gurney for so long because the paperwork was delayed and because the state's technicians had trouble finding a vein." David Thomas, director of health services for the Florida Department of Corrections, said the state "did nothing wrong." He added that "a minor surgical procedure may sometimes be necessary to locate a vein. Such a procedure could take a considerable amount of time." He insisted that "the execution was carried out in a professional manner. The inmate suffered no undue discomfort."[16]

Killers Should Suffer

Just how much discomfort should be considered undue? Linda Kelley of Houston, Texas, was the first family survivor permitted under a new state law to be present at the February 1966 execution of the murderer of her two children. The victims were her son, Mark, twenty-six years old with two children of his own, and her daughter, Kara, age twenty. Ms. Kelley thought the execution was not harsh enough.[17]

"I would like to have seen him humiliated a bit," she said when it was over. "My son dies after being shot in the face and choking on his own blood. We make it too easy."[18]

Florida Senator Ron Silver, a Democrat from North Miami Beach, opposed the state switching from the electric chair to lethal injection because he thought it "too easy of a way" to punish killers. Execution of those who take a person's life, he said "ought to be different. It ought to be extreme. Some people say, 'You want revenge.' I do."[19]

Richard W. Byrne witnessed the December 1999 execution of Andre Graham in Virginia. Graham had been convicted of cold-bloodedly killing a twenty-year-old woman while stealing a car. Byrne posted an account of the execution on a pro-death penalty Web page. He clocked the time it took the state to carry out Graham's sentence at nine minutes. He concluded that "there was nothing barbaric about the execution of Mr. Graham."[20]

Death Chamber Stress

The attitude of the law enforcement officers and prison guards present at the Graham execution was also described by Byrne. He wrote of them that they did not convey "any sense of blood lust or mindless vengeance at work, but a strong sense of people who were here to witness someone getting what they deserved." After Graham had been put to death, Byrne elicited comments from them. They all agreed with the one who said that "for what he did, [Graham] got off easy."[21]

A different sort of reaction had been witnessed by Byrne shortly before the execution took place. One of the guards appeared to Byrne to be "stressed out by the situation." He was "biting his lip" and seemed to be "about to break down in tears."[22]

Such a response may not be unusual. Warden Jim Willett, who oversees the execution chamber in Huntsville, Texas, says that he wonders "whether people really understand what goes on down here, and the effect it has on us." Kenneth Dean, an officer in the Huntsville unit, points out that "it's kind of hard to explain what you actually feel when you talk to a man, and you kind of get to know that person, and then you walk him out of a cell and you take him in there to the chamber and tie him down, and then a few minutes later he's gone."[23]

Prison chaplain Reverend Carroll Pickett believes the stress of trying to provide spiritual solace to the ninety-five prisoners he counseled prior to their execution contributed to his heart condition, which led to his triple-bypass operation. He believes stress is common among those who participate in executions. "It affects anybody," he says.[24]

Fred Allen took part in 130 executions. He was one of those who strapped the condemned prisoners to the gurney. In 2000 he was recovering from a nervous breakdown. He is concerned for those who still work on death row and are part of the execution procedure. "I want people to understand what they're going through," he says. "I don't want what happened to me to happen to them."[25]

The Function of Doctors

Few people are as qualified to understand such effects as the medical personnel who choose to be involved in executions. In different states, the services of doctors, psychologists, nurses, medical technicians, and other health care providers have been a part of the lethal injection execution process. The extent to which they are involved varies from state to state.

A psychologist or psychiatrist may be present to assure that condemned inmates are mentally competent as the law says they must be before they can be executed. Physicians may prescribe dosages or help prepare the drugs used in lethal injections to suit the body weight and physical condition of the person to be executed. Nurses and/or medical technicians may assist with locating veins that won't collapse or with inserting needles into them. The role of doctors may be advisory; they may direct the prison personnel who perform the execution procedures. Nurses and medical technicians may be members of the prison staff charged with carrying out the death sentence.[26]

The law requires that a doctor be present at all executions to pronounce death. At the same time, the physician's Hippocratic oath pledges him or her "above all to do no harm," and the American Medical Association (AMA) has said that no doctor should "be a participant in a legally authorized execution."[27] Yet no execution can take place without a doctor being present to pronounce the subject dead. If the subject isn't dead, then the doctor must give the order for further lethal injections. His order restarts the execution.

Whether medical personnel are there to ensure that death is not unduly painful or cruel, or whether their presence marks them as active accomplices to the execution, is a question usually decided by one's attitude to the death penalty itself. Most of those who favor it see the function of such professionals as insurance that the execution is carried out in a humane fashion. Those opposed accuse medical personnel of actively collaborating in state-sanctioned murder. It is part of the larger question that hangs over the death chamber: Should a civilized society kill its killers?

Afterword

Should society kill its killers? Some states that use lethal injection pay a fee to an executioner who releases the potassium chloride into the tube leading to the condemned person's vein, the action that stops the heart. Most states, however, administer lethal injections so that no one person involved in the procedure may be said to have "killed" the condemned person. Nobody involved knows which drug they have released, or the effect of their particular action. There is no one executioner. Different people perform the separate tasks of shackling the prisoner to the gurney preparing the substances used in the lethal injections, inserting the intravenous catheters, connecting the vials of substances to the catheters, turning different valves to start their flow, checking the person's heartbeat, and pronouncing him or her dead. This is meant to spare the individual the guilt of being responsible for killing the condemned person.

Responsibility is at the core of the capital punishment debate: the responsibility of the killer for his deed;

the responsibility of the police and the legal system to see that the suspected killer is treated fairly and receives a fair trial; the responsibility of the jury to render fair judgments and sentences; the responsibility of those who carry out the sentence to do so humanely; and, finally, the responsibility of all of us to ponder and decide if the death of killers is in the best interests of society.

The Execution of Timothy McVeigh

Whether or not capital punishment is in the best interests of society is a concern beyond the borders of the United States. It is a matter that aroused international protests on June 11, 2001, when the United States government executed Timothy McVeigh by lethal injection. McVeigh had been found guilty of bombing the Alfred P. Murrah Federal Building in Oklahoma City on April 19, 1995. The explosion killed 168 people, including 19 children.

Opinion in the United States strongly favored McVeigh's execution. That was not so in Europe, where virtually every country outlaws capital punishment. President Bush, beginning a European tour when the execution took place, was greeted by thousands of anti-death-penalty demonstrators in Madrid, Spain. There were similar protests scheduled in Great Britain, France, and Germany.

In the state of Oklahoma, where the bombing occurred, citizens have always been strongly pro-death penalty. Most relatives of the victims of the bombing favored putting McVeigh to death. Many felt it was necessary to provide closure to their tragedy. However, newspaper reports indicated that those who watched the execution on closed circuit television found little solace in McVeigh's death. Some of the survivors of the blast—Bud Welch, whose daughter was killed; Tim McCarthy, who lost his father; and Patti Hall, who was disabled by the explosion—were not in favor of executing McVeigh. Ms. Hall, whose bones were broken in forty places in the bombing, said, "there's been enough death."[1]

The Question

"Capital punishment," writes Russell Kirk in his book *Reclaiming a Patriarchy*, "possesses certain merciful aspects. It may be merciful . . . in that it may relieve a depraved criminal of the horror of being what he is."[2] Others believe that mercy is a matter of not killing murderers as they have killed their victims. However, what mercy is when it comes to justice is difficult to decide. As William Shakespeare wrote—

> *Though justice be thy plea, consider this,*
> *That in the course of justice, none of us*
> *Should see salvation: we do pray for mercy,*
> *And that same prayer doth teach us all to render*
> *The deeds of mercy.*[3]

But are those "deeds of mercy" the peace of death? Or are they the gift of life in prison? The question remains.

Chronology

1792	The guillotine is developed by Dr. Joseph-Ignace Guillotin.
1840	*New York Tribune* publisher and presidential candidate Horace Greeley campaigns against capital punishment.
1847	Michigan becomes the first state to abolish the death penalty. Maine and Iowa follow, but then restore it.
1887	Maine again abolishes the death penalty.
August 1890	The electric chair is used for the first time at Auburn State Prison in New York.
1907–1917	Nine states and Puerto Rico do away with capital punishment.
1921	During the previous four years, five of the nine states restore capital punishment.
1947	There are 152 executions in the United States, a high for the decade.
1954	*Cell 2455, Death Row*, written by convicted murderer Caryl Chessman, is published.

1958	The film *I Want To Live* is released and fuels public opposition to the death penalty.
May 1960	Despite worldwide protests, Caryl Chessman is executed.
1968	There is a nationwide suspension of the death penalty, which lasts for nine years.
1972	The United States Supreme Court rules that "capital punishment laws, as enforced, were unconstitutional."
1976	The Supreme Court reinstitutes the death penalty.
January 1977	Gary Gilmore is executed by a Utah firing squad, the first execution in the United States in ten years.
1982	The first execution by lethal injection takes place in Texas.
1992	Presidential candidate Governor Bill Clinton returns to Arkansas to sign papers allowing the execution of a brain-damaged murderer to proceed.
1994	The Federal Death Penalty Act, authorizing death sentences for more than sixty federal offenses, becomes law.
1995	Congress cuts off funding for twenty Death Penalty Resource Centers.
1996	The Anti-Terrorism and Effective Death Penalty Act, limiting the number of appeals in death penalty cases, is passed.
1998	Two boys, age eleven and thirteen, kill five people and wound thirteen others in Jonesboro, Arkansas.
1998	Texas Governor George W. Bush declines to stop the execution of Karla Faye Tucker despite worldwide protests.

January 1999	A nationwide *Chicago Tribune* study finds prosecutorial misconduct in 381 death-penalty cases.
April 1999	Two adolescents murder thirteen people, wound twenty-eight, and then kill themselves at Columbine High School in Littleton, Colorado.
November 1999	Wisconsin Senator Russ Feingold introduces a Senate bill to abolish the federal death penalty and requests a halt to state executions.
January 2000	Illinois Governor George H. Ryan halts all executions in his state because the capital punishment system is "fraught with errors."
February 2000	Vermont Senator Patrick Leahy introduces the Innocence Protection Act preventing the destruction of DNA evidence, which might be used in death sentence appeals.
May 2000	New Hampshire state senate passes a bill banning the death penalty, but Governor Jeanne Shaheen vetoes it.
June 2000	Gary Graham is executed despite his case emerging as an issue in the presidential campaign of Texas Governor George W. Bush.
September 2000	A U.S. Justice Department review finds bias in the administration of the federal death penalty.
June 11, 2001	Timothy McVeigh, whose 1995 bombing of the Oklahoma City Federal Building claimed 168 lives, is executed by lethal injection.

Chapter Notes

CHAPTER ONE

1. *The Mikado*, Act II, "A More Humane Mikado." Internet: www.stcloudstate.edu/~scogdill/mikado/humane-mikado.html
2. David Isay and Stacy Abramson, "No. 587: A Death Row Inmate Tells His Own Life Story," *The New York Times Magazine*, January 2, 2000, p. 34.
3. Ibid.
4. *Newsweek*, June 12, 2000, p. 26.
5. Author uncredited, "Californians Split Between Death, Life Without Parole," *The Arizona Daily Star*, January 19, 2000, section A, p. 14.
6. *Newsweek*, p. 34.
7. NAACP Legal Defense and Education Fund, "Death Row USA," Winter 2000. Internet: www.dpio.org/death_row/US_Death_Row_Statistics.html
8. Caitlin Lovinger, "Death Row's Living Alumni," *The New York Times*, August 22, 1999, pp. 1, 4.
9. Peter Slavin, "Activist's Training Helps Cheat Death Verdicts," *National Association of Social Workers News*, April 2000. Internet: www.naswpress.org/publications/news/0400/verdicts.htm

10. Benjamin Wallace-Wells, "States Follow Illinois Lead on Death Penalty," *The Boston Globe*, February 9, 2000, p. A3.
11. U.S. Death Row Statistics from NAACP Legal Defense and Education Fund provided by Death Penalty Institute of Oklahoma. Internet: www.dpio.org/death_row/ US_Death_Row_Statistics.html
12. John Kifner, "A State Votes to End Its Death Penalty," *The New York Times*, May 19, 2000, p. A16.
13. Wallace-Wells.
14. Fox Butterfield, "Death Sentences Being Overturned in 2 of 3 Appeals," *The New York Times*, June 12, 2000, p. A 1; James Q. Wilson, "What Death Penalty Errors?" *The New York Times*, July 10, 2000, Op-Ed. p. A19.
15. Wilson.
16. Lovinger, p. 1.
17. Alison Mitchell, "Gore Backs Delay in U.S. Execution, but No Wide Moratorium," *The New York Times*, July 8, 2000, p. A10.
18. Adam Clymer and Marjorie Connelly, "Poll Finds Delegates to the Left of Both Public and Party," *The New York Times*, August 14, 2000, p. A19.
19. Frank Bruni, "2 Men, Fates Linked," *The New York Times*, June 21, 2000, p. A20; Jim Yardley, "Texas' Busy Death Chamber Helps Define Bush's Tenure," *The New York Times*, January 7, 2000, p. A1; Sara Rimer and Raymond Bonner, "Bush Candidacy Puts Focus on Executions," *The New York Times*, May 14, 2000, p. 1.
20. Mike Farrell, "Death Penalty Politics," *The Nation*, July 24, 2000, p. 6.
21. Yardley, p. A13.
22. "Death Penalty Troubles in Texas," editorial, *The New York Times*, June 19, 2000, p. A18; "Irreversible Error in Texas," editorial, *The New York Times*, June 23, 2000, p. A22.
23. Author uncredited, "One Step Farther From Death," *The New York Times Week in Review*, August 27, 2000, p. wk3.
24. Frank Bruni, "Bush Stands Firm on Upholding Death Penalty," *The New York Times*, June 22, 2000, p. A28; Sara Rimer with Jim Yardley, "Pending Execution in Texas

Spotlights a Powerful Board," *The New York Times*, June 21, 2000, p. A1.
25. Bruni.
26. Frank Bruni with Jim Yardley, "With Bush Assent, Convict Executed," *The New York Times*, June 23, 2000, p. A 18.
27. Jim Yardley, "In Death Row Dispute, a Witness Stands Firm," *The New York Times*, June 16, 2000, p. A22.

CHAPTER TWO
1. Ella Wheeler Wilcox, *Settle the Question Right* in *Bartlett's Familiar Quotations*, Fourteenth Edition (Boston: Little Brown and Company, 1968), p. 826a.
2. "The Supreme Court and Individual Rights," (Washington, DC: Congressional Quarterly, Inc., 1980), p. 288.
3. Carl Sifakis, *The Encyclopedia of American Crime* (New York: Facts On File, 1982), p. 142.
4. Ibid.
5. Ibid.
6. Leslie Halliwell, *Halliwell's Film Guide* (New York: Charles Scribner's Sons, 1987), p. 501.
7. Sifakis, pp. 292–293.
8. Ibid., p. 121.
9. *Encyclopaedia Britannica*, Vol. II (Chicago: Encyclopaedia Britannica, Inc., 1984), p. 536.
10. "The Supreme Court and Individual Rights."
11. Ibid., p. 208.
12. Ibid., p. 209.
13. Ibid., p. 288.
14. Sifakis, p. 283.
15. Yale University, "The Death Sentence Remains a Question: McCleskey *v.* Kemp." Internet: www.yale.edu/ynhti/curriculum/units/1995/3/95.03.09.x.html
16. McCleskey *v.* Kemp, 481 U.S. 279 (1987). Internet: www.kwaku.org/rm/mcclesky.html
17. Amnesty International: "The U.S. Supreme Court Ignoring the Reality." Internet: www.amnestyusa.org/rightsforall/dp/race/race-4.html
18. Ibid.
19. Jennifer N. Ide for Emory University, "The Case of

Exzavious Lee Gibson: a Georgia Court's (Constitutional?) Denial of a Federal Right." Internet: www.law.emory.edu/ELJ/volumes/sum98/ide.html

20. ACLU Briefing Paper No. 8, "The Death Penalty." Internet: www.aclu.org/library/pbp8.html

21. Amnesty International Report, March 1997, "United States of America Death Penalty Developments in 1996." Internet: www.amnesty.org/ailib/aipub/1997/AMR/25100197.htm

C‍HAPTER T‍HREE

1. Exodus, *Holy Bible*, Masonic Edition (Philadelphia: A. J. Holman Company, 1940), 21:12, p. 76.

2. The National Organization of Parents of Murdered Children (POMC). Internet: info@pomc,com/popup.cfm; Death Penalty and Sentencing Information in the United States. Internet: www.prodeathpenalty.com/dp.html

3. Rutgers Lecture 7 Criminology, March 9, 1999, "Cultural and Subcultural Factors in Criminality." Internet: www.rci.rutgers.edu/~jtoby/LEC7CRIM-99.txt

4. Justice For All: "Once a murderer . . ." Internet: www.prodeathpenalty.com/repeat_murder.htm

5. Ibid.

6. Arlen Specter, "A Swifter Death Penalty Would Be An Effective Deterrent," *The Death Penalty: Opposing Viewpoints* (San Diego: Greenhaven Press, Inc., 1997), p. 116.

7. Steven E. Landsburg, "The Death Penalty Is a Deterrent," *Forbes*, November 21, 1994, *The Death Penalty: Opposing Viewpoints* (San Diego: Greenhaven Press, Inc., 1997), p.105.

8. Thomas Sowell and John J. DiJulio Jr., "The Death Penalty Is a Deterrent," *The Death Penalty: Opposing Viewpoints* (San Diego: Greenhaven Press, Inc., 1997), p. 104.

9. John P. Conrad and Ernest van den Haag, *The Death Penalty: A Debate* (New York: Plenum Press, 1983), p. 142.

10. Death Penalty and Sentencing Information in the United States. Internet: www.prodeathpenalty.com/dp.html

11. Ernest van den Haag, "Justice, Deterrence and the Death Penalty," *America's Experiment With Capital Punishment* (Durham, NC: Carolina Academic Press, 1998), pp. 144–145.
12. Bob Greene, "Who Weeps for the Blood of the Weiler Family?" *Chicago Tribune*, July 14, 1999. Internet: *Justice For All* info@prodeathpenalty.com
13. Marc Klaas, "Voices From the Front: I'll Be There to Watch My Twelve-Year-Old Daughter's Murderer Go Down," *Newsweek*, June 12, 2000, p. 35.
14. Margaret Vandiver, "The Impact of the Death Penalty on the Families of Homicide Victims and of Condemned Prisoners," *America's Experiment With Capital Punishment* (Durham, NC: Carolina Academic Press, 1998), p. 485.
15. Mike Munden, "The Death Penalty and Wilfred Berry," *The Columbus Dispatch*, February 1999. Internet: www.dispatch.com/news/newsfea99/feb99/berry/berry-home.html
16. Anonymous, "The Death Penalty: We Need It," *Related Quotations About the Death Penalty*. Internet: www.rnet.net/impeach/the death.htm
17. "Death Penalty and Sentencing Information in the United States." Internet: www.prodeathpenalty.com/dp.html
18. Ibid.

CHAPTER FOUR

1. Hugo Adam Bedau, *The Case Against The Death Penalty*, p. 16. Internet: sun.soci.niu.edu/~critcrim/dp/dppapers/aclu/anti...
2. Exodus, *Holy Bible*, Masonic Edition (Philadelphia: A. J. Holman Company, 1940), 20:13, p. 75.
3. Robert McClory, "How I Came to Forgive the Unforgivable," *U.S. Catholic* magazine, August 1998. Internet: www.uscatholic.org/1998/08/forgive.htm
4. Ibid.
5. Ibid.
6. Margaret Vandiver, "The Impact of the Death Penalty on the Families of Homicide Victims and of Condemned

Prisoners," *America's Experiment With Capital Punishment* (Durham, NC: Carolina Academic Press, 1998), p. 488.

7. Ibid., p. 486.
8. Ibid., p. 487.
9. Hugo Adam Bedau, p. 5, quoting Cochran, Chamlin and Seth, *Deterrence or Brutalization* in *Criminology*, 1994.
10. Ibid., p. 3.
11. Ibid., p. 5.
12. Bedau, p.3, quoting Dieter, Death Penalty Information Center, *On the Front Line*, 1995, p. 2.
13. USA: The Death Penalty: Briefing (Amnesty International, 1987), p. 18.
14. Bedau, quoting Dieter, p. 19.
15. "The Death Penalty List of Abolitionist and Retentionist Countries," (Amnesty International, Revised December 18, 1999). Internet: www.amnesty.org/ailib/intcam/dp/abrelist.htm
16. "Justice For All: Info and Resources." Internet: info@prodeathpenalty.com
17. Ibid.; "Fatal Flaws: Innocence and Death Penalty in the USA" (Amnesty International). Internet: www.amnesty-usa.org/rightsforall/dp/innocense/innocent-2.html
18. "Thanks to Modern Science . . ." (ACLU ad), *New Yorker*, September 25, 2000, p. 23.
19. Fatal Flaws.
20. "The Supreme Court and Individual Rights" (Washington, D.C.: Congressional Quarterly, Inc., 1980), p. 288.
21. Raymond Bonner and Ford Fessenden, "States With No Death Penalty Share Lower Homicide Rates," *The New York Times*, September 22, 2000, p. A23.
22. Robert M. Bohm, "The Economic Costs of Capital Punishment: Past, Present, and Future," *America's Experiment With Capital Punishment* (Durham, NC: Carolina Academic Press, 1998), p. 439.
23. Bonner and Fessenden, p. A1.

CHAPTER FIVE

1. Wade Butler, letter to the editor, *The New York Times*, February 5, 2000, p. A14.

2. Ernest van den Haag, "Justice, Deterrence and the Death Penalty," *America's Experiment With Capital Punishment* (Durham, NC: Carolina Academic Press, 1998), p. 148.

3. Sir William Blackstone, *Commentaries, Book IV, Chapter 27, Bartlett's Familiar Quotations*, 14th ed. (Boston: Little Brown and Company, 1968), p. 444 b.

4. Angel Fire: "The Risk of Execution." Internet: www.angelfire.com/la/michaelbruno/innocent.html

5. Ibid.

6. Ibid.

7. Ibid.

8. *Newsweek*, June 12, 2000, p. 31.

9. Ibid.; Pro-Death Penalty: "September 2000 Executions." Internet: info@prodeathpenalty.com/Pending/00/sep00.htm

10. *Newsweek*.

11. Ibid., p. 26.

12. "September 2000 Executions."

13. *Encyclopaedia Britannica*, Vol. III (Chicago: Encyclopaedia Britannica, Inc., 1984), p. 473; Jean L. McKechnie, ed., *Webster's New Universal Unabridged Dictionary*, 2nd ed. (New York: Dorset & Baber, 1983), p. 539.

14. *Newsweek*, p. 32.

15. Ibid.

16. Ibid., p. 28.

17. Wayne F. Smith, "The Justice Project" (solicitation letter), p. 3.

18. Ibid.; News Release, Gordon H. Smith, United States Senator for Oregon, "Senators Smith & Leahy Reintroduce Innocence Protection Act." Internet: www.senate.gov/~gsmith/press/000607.htm

19. Peter Neufeld and Barry Scheck, "Better Ways to Find the Guilty," *The New York Times*, June 5, 2000, op. ed., p. A21.

20. Death Penalty Institute of Oklahoma, Robert Peebles, "Review: Actual Innocence," October 2, 2000. Internet: www.dpio.org/bookstore/Actual_Innocence.html

21. Ibid.

22. George F. Will, "Innocent on Death Row," *The Washington Post*, April 6, 2000, p. A23. Internet: washing-

tonpost.com/wp-dyn/articles/A20906-2000Apr5.html
23. Francis X. Clines, "Virginia Man Is Pardoned in a Murder; DNA Is Cited," *The New York Times*, October 3, 2000, p. A18.
24. Ibid.
25. Ibid.
26. "The New Death Penalty Politics," editorial, *The New York Times*, June 7, 2000, p. A30.
27. John Schank Letter to the Editor, *Newsweek*, July 3, 2000, p. 14.

CHAPTER SIX

1. John Locke, *Essay Concerning Human Understanding*, Book 20, Chapter 17, *Bartlett's Familiar Quotations*, 14th ed. (Boston: Little Brown and Company, 1968), p. 372.
2. Tena Jamison Lee, "Anatomy of a Death Penalty Case," *Human Rights*, Vol. 23, No. 3, Summer 1996. Internet: www.abanet.org/irr/hr/anatomy.html
3. Ibid.
4. Ibid.
5. Ibid.
6. "Judge John T. Nixon and The Facts." Internet: www.rnet/impeach/thefacts.htm
7. Ibid.
8. Ibid.
9. Stephen B. Bright, "The Politics of Capital Punishment: The Sacrifice of Fairness for Executions," *America's Experiment With Capital Punishment* (Durham, NC: Carolina Academic Press, 1998), pp. 123–124.
10. "Prosecutorial Misconduct," *Chicago Tribune*. Internet: www.capdefnet.org/current.htm
11. Ibid.; Maurice Posley and Ken Armstrong, "Prosecution on Trial in DuPage," *Chicago Tribune*, January 12, 1999. Internet: chicagotribune.com/news/nationworld/ws/item/0,1308,21398-21579-21577,00.html
12. Possley and Armstrong.
13. Ibid.
14. Ibid.

15. Ibid.
16. Ibid.
17. Maurice Possley and Ken Armstrong, "The Verdict: Dishonor," *Chicago Tribune*, January 8, 1999. Internet: chicagotribune.com/news/nationworld/ws/item/0,1308,21 398-21420-21467,00.html
18. Sara Rimer and Raymond Bonner, "Texas Lawyer's Death Row Record a Concern," *The New York Times*, June 11, 2000, pp. A1, 26.
19. Ibid.
20. Ibid.
21. Ibid.
22. Sara Rimer, "Questions of Death Row Justice for Poor People in Alabama," *The New York Times*, March 1, 2000, pp. A1, A16.
23. Joseph P. Fried, "District Attorneys Are Providing Mutual Aid in Death Penalty Cases," *The New York Times*, November 21, 1999, pp. 45, 47.
24. Rimer, "Questions of Death Row Justice for Poor People in Alabama."
25. Ibid.
26. Ibid.
27. Susan Blaustein, "Habeus Corpus Has Been Undermined by the Supreme Court," *The Death Penalty: Opposing Viewpoints* (San Diego: Greenhaven Press, Inc., 1997), p. 131.
28. Bryan A. Stevenson, "State Courts and Capital Defendants: The Point," *The Death Penalty and the Disadvantaged* (Hudson, Wisconsin: Gem Publications, Inc., 1997), p. 87.
29. Marla Sandys, "Stacking the Deck for Guilt and Death: The Failure of Death Qualification to Ensure Impartiality," *America's Experiment With Capital Punishment* (Durham, NC: Carolina Academic Press, 1998), p. 285.
30. Ibid., pp. 288–289, 295.
31. "Capital Punishment Decisions Hinge on Jurors Who May Not Understand Their Task" (National Science Foundation), *NSF News*. Internet: www.nsf.gov/od/lpa/news/press/pr972.htm

32. "Death Penalty Articles," *Justice: Denied—The Magazine for the Wrongly Convicted.* Internet: www.justicedenied.org/deathpenalty.htm
33. Ibid.

CHAPTER SEVEN

1. "Teenager Who Killed Teacher Says He Didn't Mean to Shoot," *The Washington Post,* September 12, 2000, p. A7.
2. Jennifer Gonnerman, "Kids on the Row," *The Village Voice,* January 11, 2000, p. 47; "The Ultimate Injustice," editorial, *Boston Globe,* August 24, 2000, p. A16.
3. Amnesty International, "Executing Children Is an Unnecessary Practice," *The Death Penalty and the Disadvantaged* (Hudson, WI: Gem Publications, Inc., 1997), p. 137.
4. Gonnerman.
5. James J. Kilpatrick, "Executing Children: Let The States Decide What Is Cruel And Unusual," *The Death Penalty and the Disadvantaged* (Hudson, WI: Gem Publications, Inc., 1997), p. 142.
6. Steven A. Drizin and Stephen K. Harper, "Old Enough to Kill, Old Enough to Die," *San Francisco Chronicle,* April 16, 2000, pp. 4–5.
7. Ibid., p. 4.
8. Ibid.
9. Kimberly Lamke, "Why Boy Was Suffocated Remains Mystery," *Houston Chronicle,* August 27, 2000, p. 17; Leonard Pitts, "Amid Terrible Tragedy, a Glimmer of Hope," *Denver Post,* August 27, 2000, p. K-02.
10. "Teenager Who Killed Teacher Says He Didn't Mean to Shoot."
11. Brett Blackwell, "It's Easier to Blame Guns than Individuals," *Buffalo News,* June 20, 2000, p. B 3.
12. "Tolerant Society, Youth No Excuse to Pardon 'Jonesboro Massacre' Boys," March 27, 1998. Internet: www.southend.wayne.edu/archive/archdate/327/forum/jones/jones.html; "Boy Shooters Guilty in Jonesboro Massacre," *The Holland Sentinel,* August 12, 1998. Internet: www.thehollandsentinel.net/stories/o81298/new_boys.html

13. Jim Hughes, "Massacre at Columbine High: Descriptions Vary of Suspects," *The Denver Post Online*, October 12, 2000. Internet: www.denverpost.com/news/shot 0420d.htm; Mark Obmascik, "Bloodbath Leaves Fifteen Dead, Twenty-Eight Hurt," *The Denver Post Online*, 10/12/00. Internet: www.denverpost.com/news/shot 0420a.htm
14. Obmascik.
15. Drizin and Harper, p. 3.
16. "More Texas Executions," editorial, *The New York Times*, August 9, 2000, p. A 26.
17. "Man Said to Be Retarded Is One of Two Killers Executed," *The New York Times*, August 10, 2000, p. A17; Raymond Bonner and Sara Rimer, "Executing the Mentally Retarded Even as Laws Begin to Shift," *The New York Times*, August 7, 2000, p. A1.
18. John Derbyshire, "She Was Just Someone," *National Review Online*, October 13, 2000. Internet: www.nationalreview.com/nr_comment/nr_comment081000b.shtml
19. "More Texas Executions."
20. Derbyshire.
21. Bonner and Rimer.

CHAPTER EIGHT

1. Mumia Abu-Jamal, *Live from Death Row* (New York: Avon Books, 1995), p. 28.
2. Francis X. Clines, "The Poster Boy for and Against the Death Penalty," *The New York Times*, May 21, 2000, p. 3.
3. Ibid.; C. Clark Kissinger, "Legal Update on Mumia: The State of the Legal Battle to Save Mumia's Life," October 11, 2000. Internet: www.iacenter.org/maj_leg101100.htm
4. "Philadelphia Online: Mumia Abu-Jamal." Internet: www.philly.com/packages/mumia/html/inq072395.asp
5. Ibid.
6. "The Case of Mumia Abu-Jamal," October 16, 2000. Internet: www.freezone.co.uk/liberationmag/mumia.htm
7. Ibid.; "What Are the Facts in the Case of Mumia Abu-Jamal?" (New York Free Mumia Abu-Jamal Coalition, October 16, 2000). Internet: www.multimania.com/jsr4/dossiers/mumia/facts.html

8. "The Case of Mumia Abu-Jamal," October 16, 2000. Internet: www.freezone.co.uk/liberationmag/mumia.htm
9. Richard C. Dieter, Esq., "The Death Penalty in Black & White: Who Lives, Who Dies, Who Decides" (Washington, DC: Death Penalty Information Center, October 17, 2000), Internet: www.deathpenaltyinfo.org/racerpt.html; "The Death Penalty" (ACLU Briefing Paper No. 8), p. 2. Internet: pbp8.html at www.aclu.org
10. Dieter.
11. "National Implications: Race and the Death Penalty" (Death Penalty Information Center). Internet: www.deathpenaltyinfo.org/dpic.r04.html
12. Wesley Lowe, "Racism and Capital Punishment" (Wesley Lowe's Pro Death Penalty Web page). Internet: www.geocities.com/Area51/Capsule/2698/cp.html
13. Stanley Rothman and Stephen Powers, "The Death Penalty Is Not Applied Unfairly to Blacks," *The Death Penalty: Opposing Viewpoints* (San Diego: Greenhaven Press, Inc., 1997), p. 160.
14. Wayne Woolley, "Crime: More Blacks Are Backing Capital Punishment Now: Fears Escalate Even as Crime Rates Drop in Detroit and Other Cities," *The Detroit News*, October 11, 1996. Internet: detnews.com/1996/menu/stories/69081.htm
15. Ibid.
16. Dieter.
17. Ibid., p.14.
18. Raymond Bonner and Marc Lacey, "Pervasive Disparities Found in the Federal Death Penalty," *The New York Times*, September 12, 2000, p. A18; *The Death Penalty* (ACLU Briefing Paper No. 8). Internet: pbp8.html at www.aclu.org

CHAPTER NINE
1. Bob Dylan, *A Hard Rain's A-Gonna Fall.* Internet: members.aol.com/Pjuddy/bum/a_hard_r.htm
2. Stephen Hunter, "The Sad, Sad World Of 'Mr. Death,'" *The Washington Post*, March 10, 2000, p. C5; James Berardinelli, "Mr. Death: The Rise and Fall of Fred A.

Leuchter   Jr."   Internet: movie-reviews.colossus.net/
movies/m/mr_death.html

3. Ibid.

4. Ibid.

5. *Encyclopaedia   Brittanica*,   Book   4   (Chicago:
   Encyclopaedia Britannica, Inc., 1984), p. 788.

6. Ibid.

7. Kari Haskell, "Never Say Die. Just Execute," *The New
   York Times*, July 23, 2000, p. 3.

8. Helen Prejean, C.S.J., *Dead Man Walking: An Eyewitness
   Account of the Death Penalty in the United States* (New
   York: Random House, 1993), p. 18.

9. Michael L. Radelet, "Post-Furman Botched Executions"
   (Death   Penalty   Information   Center).   Internet:
   www.essential.org/dpic/botched.html

10. "Additional Execution Information," October 10, 2000
    (Death Penalty Information Center) Internet: www.death-
    penaltyinfo.org/dpicexec.html; "Methods of Execution,"
    October 23, 2000. Internet: www.prodeathpenalty.com/
    methods.htm

11. "Methods of Execution," October 23, 2000. Internet:
    www.prodeathpenalty.com/methods.htm

12. Ibid.

13. Hugo Adam Bedau, "The Case Against the Death Penalty"
    (ACLU). Internet: www.aclu.org/library/case_against_
    death.html

14. Rick Bragg, "Florida Inmate Claimed Abuse in
    Execution," *The New York Times*, June 9, 2000, p. A14.

15. Ibid.

16. Ibid.

17. "The Place for Vengeance," *U.S. News & World Report*,
    June 17, 1997. Internet: www.prodeathpenalty.com/
    vengeance.htm

18. Ibid.

19. Jim Saunders and Randolph Pendleton, "Lawmakers Vote
    Changes in Executions: Lethal Injection Improved,"
    Florida Times Union, January 7, 2000. Internet: jack-
    sonville.com/tu-online/stories/010700/met_1732647.html

20. Richard W. Byrne, "Witness to an Execution," December
    9, 1999. Internet: www.prodeathpenalty.com/witness.htm

21. Ibid.

22. Ibid.

23. Bob Herbert, "Death Penalty Victims," *The New York Times*, October 12, 2000, p. A29.

24. Ibid.

25. Ibid.

26. Charles Patrick Ewing, "Above All, Do No Harm: The Role of Health and Mental Health Professionals in the Capital Punishment Process," *America's Experiment With Capital Punishment* (Durham, NC: Carolina Academic Press, 1998), pp. 461–474.

27. Ibid., p. 461; Ruling of the *American Medical Association's House of Delegates, 1980.*

AFTERWORD

1. Sara Rimer, "Victims Not of One Voice on Execution of McVeigh," *The New York Times*, April 25, 2001, p. A16.

2. Jamers L. Sauer, "The Cure of Bloody Souls," *New American*, August 30, 1990. Internet: www.thenewamerican.com/focus/cap_punishment/vo06no17_cure.htm

3. William Shakespeare, *The Merchant of Venice*, IV, i, 184, *Bartlett's Familiar Quotations*, 14th ed. (Boston: Little Brown and Company, 1968), p. 234 b.

Glossary

appeal—the request to a higher court to set aside either the verdict or the sentence of a lower court

autopsy—medical examination of a dead body

capital crime—an offense punishable by death

capital punishment—the execution of convicted felons for murder or other crimes

closure—the acceptance of the death by violence of a loved one

condemned—sentenced to be executed

"cruel and unusual punishment"—the phrase in the Eighth Amendment to the United States Constitution, which may or may not ban the death penalty

death penalty—legal authorization to execute a convicted lawbreaker

death row—the prison cell block in which condemned inmates are held

defendant—a person accused of a crime

defense counsel—the lawyer who represents the accused person at trial

deoxyribonucleic acid (DNA)—that part of a human chromosome that positively identifies a person through samples of hair, skin, bodily fluids, etc.

deterrence—the prevention of a future crime by harshly punishing an offender

electric chair—a device designed to execute criminals by inflicting massive and successive electrical shocks

execution—the legal putting to death of a criminal

executioner—the person who carries out the sentence of death

guillotine—an execution device utilizing a weighted blade to chop off the head of the condemned

gurney—a stretcherlike padded board, sometimes on wheels, to which a person is strapped for execution by lethal injection

hanging judges—justices prone to handing down death sentences

Innocence Protection Act—the bill pending in the U.S. House of Representatives and Senate that would require the preservation of DNA evidence after trial for death-row appeals

jailhouse informants—convicts who obtain information from fellow prisoners which can be used against them in court; they usually act in exchange for a reduced sentence

law-and-order platforms—political programs that favor strong policing and sentencing measures for convicted criminals, and are usually pro-capital punishment

lethal injection—inserting deadly drugs into the bloodstream of the condemned; the most common method of execution used in the United States

"lifer"—a felon sentenced to life in jail, sometimes as an alternative to a death sentence

mentally retarded—a person with a substandard IQ, which may slow down the reasoning process, but may not interfere with telling right from wrong

mitigating circumstances—factors introduced to justify a lesser punishment

moratorium—a halt in executions for a period of time while the capital punishment system in a state or nation is examined

plea bargaining—reducing a charge against a person, often in exchange for testimony against a codefendant

prosecutorial misconduct—usually withholding of evidence helpful to a defendant's case or deliberately presenting false evidence

punishment phase—the hearing that takes place after conviction to decide the sentence

retribution (retributive justice)—punishment equal to the severity of the crime (i.e., an eye for an eye)

stay—term used when an execution is delayed for consideration of mitigating factors

superpredator—a violent and out-of-control adolescent

survivor—close family member of a murder victim

unconstitutional—not legal according to the United States Constitution

United States Supreme Court—the highest court in the land; the last court of appeal for those facing the death penalty

wrongful execution—the legal putting to death of an innocent person

youthful offender—a minor who commits a crime

For Further Information

BOOKS

Abu-Jamal, Mumia. *Live from Death Row.* New York: Avon Books, Inc., 1996.

Acker, James R., Robert M. Bohm, and Charles S. Lanier, eds. *America's Experiment with Capital Punishment.* Durham, NC: Carolina Academic Press, 1998.

Gaines, Ernest J. *A Lesson Before Dying.* New York: Alfred A. Knopf, 1997.

Gottfried, Ted. *Capital Punishment: The Death Penalty Debate.* Springfield, NJ: Enslow Publishers, Inc., 1997.

McCuen, Gary E., ed. *The Death Penalty and the Disadvantaged.* Hudson, WI: Gem Publications Inc., 1997.

McFeeley, William S. *Proximity to Death.* New York: W. W. Norton & Company, 2000.

Prejean, Helen, C. S. J. *Dead Man Walking: An Eyewitness Account of the Death Penalty in the United States.* New York: Random House, 1993.

Rhodes, Richard. *Why They Kill: The Discoveries of a Maverick Criminologist.* New York: Alfred A. Knopf, 1999.

Scott, Gini Graham, Ph.D. *Homicide: 100 Years of Murder in America.* Los Angeles: Lowell House Juvenile, 1998.

Sifakis, Carl. *The Encyclopedia of American Crime.* New York: Facts On File, 1982.

FILMS (AVAILABLE ON VIDEOCASSETTE)

Dead Man Walking, directed by Tim Robbins, 1995.

The Executioner's Song, directed by Lawrence Schiller, 1982.

I Want to Live, directed by Robert Wise, 1958.

In Cold Blood, directed by Richard Brooks, 1967.

Mr. Death: The Rise and Fall of Fred A. Leuchter Jr. (documentary), directed by Errol Morris, 1999.

INTERNET SITES (ALL HAVE LINKS TO RELATED SITES)

American Civil Liberties Union (ACLU)
www.aclu.org/death-penalty/

Amnesty International
www.amnestyusa.org

Death Penalty Information Center
www.deathpenaltyinfo.org

Justice For All
www.jfa.net/

Murder Victims Families for Reconciliation (MVFR)
www.mvfr.org/home.htm

Murder Victims.com
www.murdervictims.com/

National Center for Victims of Crime
www.nvc.org/

National Organization of Parents of Murdered Children (POMC)
www.pomc.com/

United States Department of Justice
www.usdoj.gov/

Index

Page numbers in *italics* refer to illustrations.

Abbott, Jack Henry, 37, 39
Abortion clinic bombings, 33
Abraham, Lynne, 95
Abramson, Stacy, 11
Abu-Jamal, Mumia, 92–93, *94*, 95
Adan, Richard, 39
Alabama, 77, 78, 80, 104
Alaska, 15, 31
Allen, Fred, 111
American Bar Association, 18, 83
American Orthopsychiatric Association, 82–83
Amnesty International, 19, 53, 83
Anti-terrorism and Effective Death Penalty Act of 1996, 34
Appeals, 16, 26, 34–35, 40, 45, 52, 68
Arizona, 79
Arkansas, 86, 88, 104

Barton, Corey R., 36
Bedau, Hugo Adam, 50–51
Berry, Wilford, 44
Blackstone, Sir William, 57
Blackwell, Brett, 85, 86
Blaustein, Susan, 79
Botkins, David, 16
Bowers, Michael, 58
Bowler, Richard, 44
Bradley, Bill, 16
Brazill, Nathaniel, 82, 86
Brennan, William J., 31, 53
Brinkworth, R.N., 39

British law, 24, 57
Brown, Edmund G., 26
Buckley, Stephen, 71, 72
Bush, George W., *17*, 18–19, 21–23, 61, 90–91
Bush, Jeb, 90, 91
Butler, Wade, 56, 57
Byrne, Richard W., 109–110

California, 52, 70, 85
Capital crimes, defined, 12–13
Carlisle, Peter, 54
Carter, Debra Sue, 13
CBS News, 18
Cell 2455, Death Row (Chessman), 26
Center for Wrongful Convictions and the Death Penalty, 14
Chessman, Caryl, 25–26, *27*, 28
Chicago Tribune, 14, 70, 74
Child Welfare League of America, 82
Chobert, Robert, 95
Clay, Darryl, 98
Clements, Dianne, 83
Clinton, Bill, 18, 34
Clinton, Hillary, 18
Closure, need for, 44, 78
Colorado, 25, 76, 79, 86, 88
Columbia University Law School, 15–16, 18
Columbine shooting, 86, 88
Condemned
    families of, 48, 50
    mental pain of, 53
Criminology magazine, 50–51
"Cruel and unusual punishments," 24, 31, 53
Cruz, Oliver David, 89–90

Cruz, Rolando, 71–72, *73*
Cutler, Zelma, 63

Davis, Allen Lee, 42
Davis, Richard Allen, 42
Dean, Kenneth, 110
Deans, Marie, 47
Defense attorneys, 66, 74,
    76–79
Delaware, 31, 80
Demps, Bennie, 39–40, 108–109
Derbyshire, John, 90
Deterrent, death sentences as,
    40–41, 51
DiJulio, John, 84–85
DiLisio, Tony, 67
District of Columbia, 15
DNA (deoxyribonucleic acid)
    testing, 13, 61–65
Donovan, Kelly Elizabeth, 90
Dugan, Brian, 72

Ehrlich, Isaac, 41
Eighth Amendment to the
    Constitution, 24, 31, 53, 89
Electric chair, 58, 101, 104, *105*
European Convention on
    Human Rights, Sixth
    Protocol to, 52
Executioner's Song (Mailer), 33

Families of condemned, 48, 50
Faulkner, Daniel, 93, 95
Federal Death Penalty Act of
    1994, 34
Feingold, Russ, 18
Felker, Ellis Wayne, 57–59
Financial issues, 45, 54
Firing squad, 32–33, 105
Flanary, Stephanie Rae, 59, 61
Florida, 39, 42, 52, 67–68, 70,
    80, 86, 96, 104, 108–109
Forbes magazine, 40
Fowler, Anna Laura, 63
Franklin, Benjamin, 25
Freeman, Traci, 44

Gaines, Ernest J., 99
Gallup Organization, 13
Gas chamber, 26, 28, 105

Georgia, 33–34, 57–58, 77, 104
Gilmore, Gary, 32–33, 35, 37
Gilmore, James S., III, 64–65
Golden, Andrew, *87*, 88
Gore, Al, 16, 18–19, 23
Gore, Glenn, 13
Graham, Andre, 109–110
Graham, Barbara, 28, *30*, 31,
    74, *75*, 76
Graham, Gary, 21–23
Greeley, Horace, 25
Gregg v. *Georgia* (1976), 32
Grunow, Barry, 82, 86
Guillotin, Joseph-Ignace, 102
Guillotine, 102, *103*, 104

Halliwell, Leslie, 28
Hanging, 105
Hanging judges, 66, 67–68
Harberts, Laura Lynn, 67
Harris, Eric, 88
Harris, Sally, 36
Hawaii, 15, 31, 52
Hayward, Susan, 28, *29*
Hernandez, Alejandro, 71, 72

Idaho, 79
Illinois, 14, 15, 18, 52, 71–72,
    80, 96
Indiana, 15, 80
Innocence Project, 63–65
Innocence Protection Act of
    2000, 63
Innocent people, 13–16, 53,
    56–59, 61–65, 80
International Covenant on Civil
    and Political Rights, 84
In the Belly of the Beast
    (Abbott), 37, *38*
Iowa, 15, 25
Isay, David, 11
I Want to Live (movie), 28, *29*,
    31

Jackson, Jesse, 99
Jaeger, Marietta, 47–48
Jaeger, Susie, 47, 48
Jailhouse informants, 72
Jenkins, Pamela, 95
Johnson, Mitchell, *87*, 88

Jones, Anna, 98
Jones, Veronica, 95
Jonesboro shooting, 86, 88
Juries, 80
Justice, John, 74
Justice for All (JFA), 80
Justice system, 66–81
Juvenile offenders, 82–89

Kelley, Linda, 109
Kemplin, Jerry, 90
Kentucky, 15, 104
Kilander, Robert, 71, 72, 74
Kilpatrick, James J., 83
King, Coretta Scott, 46, 47, 99
King, Martin Luther, Jr., 46
King, Patrick, 71, 72, 74
Kirk, Russell, 114
Klaas, Marc, 42, 44
Klaas, Polly, 42, *43*, 44
Klebold, Dylan, 88
Knight, Thomas, 71, 72, 74

Lamb, John Michael, 11–12
Lambert, Bobby, 21, 23
Lanagan, Patrick A., 97
Landsburg, Steven E., 40
Lazio, Rick, 18
Leahy, Patrick, 62–63
Lethal injection, 11, 53, 61, 63,
    100, 105, *107*, 108–113
Leuchter, Fred, 101–102, 104
Liebman, James, 16
Life imprisonment, 13, 39–40,
    41, 45
Locke, John, 66
Lohman, Mark, 85
Lott, Ronald, 63
Louisiana, 52, 105, 106
Ludlam, Joy, 57, 58

Mailer, Norman, 26, 33, 37
Maine, 15, 25
Mandela, Nelson, 99
Mansfield, Steven W., 70
Marshall, Lawrence, 14
Maryland, 15
Massachusetts, 15, 52
McCain, John, 18
McClesky, Warren, 33–34

McClesky v. *Kemp* (1987),
    33–34
McGinn, Ricky, 59, *60*, 61
McGregor, Robert, 67–68
McVeigh, Timothy, 114–115
Medical personnel, 111–112
Medina, Pedro, 104
Mello, Michael, 68
Mental retardation, 89–91
Merton, Shari Ann, 36
Meyers, Wilson, 77
Michigan, 15, 25, 52, 98
Miller, Robert, Jr., 63
Minnesota, 15
Mississippi, 70, 77, 96
Mitigating circumstances, 13,
    78, 79
Mitroff, Charles J., Jr., 44
Mock, Ronald G., 21, 74, 76
Montana, 47, 48, 79
Moratorium, 14–15, 18
Murder Victims Families for
    Reconciliation (MVFR), 47,
    48, *49*
Murray v. *Giarratano* (1989), 34

Nagle, Daniel, 40
National Coalition to Abolish
    the Death Penalty, 50
National Council on Crime and
    Delinquency, 82–83
National Parents and Teachers
    Association, 82
Nebraska, 79, 104
New Hampshire, 15
New Jersey, 15, 76
Newsweek magazine, 13, 65
New York, 52, 76–77, 104
New York Times, The, 15–16,
    18, 21, 55, 65, 74, 90, 92
Nicarico, Jeanine, 71, 72
Nixon, John T., 68, *69*, 70
Nixon, Richard, 32
North Carolina, 96
North Dakota, 15

Ohio, 104
Oklahoma, 15, 63, 96, 104, 115
Oklahoma City Federal Building
    bombing, 33, 114–115

Oregon, 15

Pancuronium bromide, 107
Penalty hearings, 77–78
Pennsylvania, 15, 52, 92–93,
    95–96
Pickett, Carroll, 110–111
Plea bargaining, 36, 66, 90
Pokorak, Jeffrey, 99
Potassium chloride, 107, 113
Powell, Lewis, 32, 34
Powers, Stephen, 97
Premeditation, 12, 79
Presidential campaign of 2000,
    16, *17*, 18–19
Prosecutors, 70–72, 74
Protess, David, 14
Pruett, Robert Lynn, 40
Public Policy Institute of
    California, 13
Puerto Rico, 25
Puhlick, Celia, 39
Puhlick, Nicholas, 39

Racial bias, 33–34, 92–100
Random House, 37
Red-Light Bandit, 25
Rehabilitation, 54
Retributive justice, 42, 44
Reversed convictions, 14,
    78–79
Rhode Island, 15, 25
Richards, Ann, 22
Robertson, Pat, 18
Rothman, Stanley, 97
Rush, Benjamin, 25
Ryan, George H., 14–15, 80

Sabo, Albert, 95
Sampson, Robert, 98
Schank, John, 65
Scheck, Barry C., 64
Shaheen, Jeanne, 15
Shakespeare, William, 114
Shupe, Betti, 44
Silver, Ron, 109
Skillern, Bernadine, 21, 23
Smith, Gordon, 63
Sodium thiopental, 105
South Carolina, 105

Spaziano, Joseph "Crazy Joe,"
    67–68
Specter, Arlen, 40
Stay of execution, 26, 57
Stiffler, Damien, 85
Superpredator, myth of, 85
Survivor testimony, 78

Tarver, Robert Lee, Jr., 78
Tate, Lynwood, 67
Tennessee, 68, 70, 105
Terrorism, 33, 51
Texas, 19, 21–23, 40, 52, 59, 61,
    70, 74, 76, 77, 89–91, 109,
    110
Thomas, David, 109
Todd, Evan, 88
Trevathan, Richard, 76
Tucker, Karla Faye, 19, *20*, 21

United Nations, 19, 51–52
    Convention on the Rights
    of the Child, 84
United States Supreme Court,
    15, 22, 31–34, 39, 58, 68,
    79, 83, 89, 104
Utah, 33

van den Haag, Ernest, 41, 57
Vengeance, 42, 44
Vermont, 15
Virginia, 64, 77, 105, 109–110

Washington, Earl, 64
Washington state, 15
Weiler family, 42
West Virginia, 15
White, Cynthia, 95
White, Penny, 70
Wideman, John Edgar, 99
Wilcox, Ella Wheeler, 24
Wilder, L. Douglas, 64
Wilkins, Heath, 83
Willett, Jim, 110
Williams, Rebecca, 64
Williamson, Ronald, 13–14
Wilson, James Q., 16
Wilson, Roe, 76
Wisconsin, 15, 25
World Trade Center bombing,
    33